# CHANGE AND THE CURRICULUM

*by*

DISCARDED

Geva M. Blenkin,
Gwyn Edwards and
A. V. Kelly

P·C·P
Paul Chapman
Publishing Ltd

Copyright © 1992 Geva M. Blenkin, Gwyn Edwards and A. V. Kelly

All rights reserved

Paul Chapman Publishing Ltd
144 Liverpool Road
London N1 1LA

Apart from any fair dealing for the purposes of research or private study, or criticism or review, as permitted under the Copyright, Designs and Patents Act, 1988, this publication may be reproduced, stored or transmitted, in any form or by any means, only with the prior permission in writing of the publishers, or in the case of reprographic reproduction in accordance with the terms of licences issued by the Copyright Licensing Agency. Inquiries concerning reproduction outside those terms should be sent to the publishers at the abovementioned address.

British Library Cataloguing in Publication Data
Change and the curriculum.
  I. Blenkin, Geva M.   II. Edwards, Gwyn   III. Kelly, A. V.
  373.190941

ISBN 1 85396 154 X

Typeset by Best-set Typesetter Ltd., Hong Kong.
Printed and bound by Athenaeum Press Ltd, Newcastle upon Tyne.

A B C D E F G H  9 8 7 6 5 4 3 2

# CONTENTS

# INTRODUCTION

Curriculum change has been a major feature of the educational scene for several decades in the United Kingdom – and elsewhere too – as attempts have been made to ensure that the school curriculum responds to changes occurring in the nature and values of society, and that it is able to profit from advances in our understanding of education itself and of the educational process.

Yet little consideration has been given to questions about the relation between curriculum change and changes in society. What is the role of education in a rapidly changing society? Should the curriculum respond to social change? If so, *why* should it? And, if so, *how* should it? There are several different answers that can be offered to these questions. Clearly it is unsatisfactory to set about changing the curriculum on the basis of mere assumptions, or, worse, with the intent of discouraging questioning, at this level, of policies we wish to promote or impose. The concept of change needs to be carefully explored as a basis for understanding the processes of curriculum change and for ensuring a proper and sound foundation for our developmental policies. This is one major issue this book will seek to address.

Furthermore, the practice of curriculum change during the last several decades has been accompanied by a broadening and deepening of our understanding of the processes of change in social institutions, including educational institutions. Attempts have been made to create a conceptual framework for analysing and understanding the process of educational change, and a number of different, though related, perspectives have been offered. Such attempts have revealed the conceptual complexities behind the planning of educational change, and, in doing so, they have highlighted the importance of striving for a clearer theoretical base for such planning. For, as with all aspects of educational provision, sound practice can only be achieved from a platform of sound theory. This is a second major dimension of curriculum change which this book will examine.

Third, this kind of exploration has also revealed that the mechanisms of, and strategies for, changing the curriculum have been relatively ill understood, so that much curriculum change and development has been mishandled and has lost much of its potential value and effectiveness. Indeed, in some cases it has actually been counterproductive to its own stated aims.

Yet, from failure as well as from success, much has been learnt in recent years about curriculum innovation, change and development, and about the most effective means for bringing these about. Much has also been learnt about the effects of innovations which have not been well planned and whose mechanisms of implementation have not been clearly or carefully designed. In particular, through the work of the Schools Council and other national agencies, the difficulties of achieving effective curriculum change through centralized initiatives or directives have been well documented. Those difficulties appear to be equally significant whether the national agencies and their initiatives are concerned with curriculum development, with monitoring of performance or with centralized control. For the importance of proper and genuine forms of teacher involvement in curriculum change has become apparent; and the advantages of curriculum evolution over revolutionary innovations have emerged very clearly from such experience. Hence, in recent years, much attention has been directed towards understanding and supporting curriculum development at the level of the individual school and, indeed, the individual teacher, so that various forms of school-based curriculum development or school-centred innovation have been tried and subjected to close analysis. Again, a good deal has been learnt from this, and we will be seeking in this book to outline much of what has been learnt.

This knowledge and the understandings it has generated are especially important at a time when unusually sweeping changes are being imposed upon the school curriculum, in terms of its content, in relation to the methods adopted for its 'delivery' and in the way in which it is conceived.

It is also becoming increasingly clear that curriculum change, and indeed social change, have far greater ramifications than might at first be recognized. For they lead to changes not only in the way in which we do things but also in the way in which we think about them and talk about them. Changes in our curriculum practices reflect parallel changes in our ways of viewing and conceptualizing curriculum. And so they are also associated with new points of focus for debate, with new forms of language and imagery and with new forms of discourse. Whether these new forms precede or follow changes in practice, is an important question. And what is equally important is whether this relationship is used by those who wish to impose certain practices and changes on teachers, schools or society; whether changing the nature of the discourse of the educational debate is not the most effective device available to them for changing educational practice; and whether this is a legitimate device to use in a society which claims to be democratic. This is a further issue which this book will address.

The book sets out to draw together the many strands of the understandings which have emerged from recent studies of curriculum change in order to make them available in a coherent and compelling form. It is intended for those who wish to change the school curriculum, whether in particular subject areas or *in toto*, and who wish to do this in such a way as to ensure that the changes they seek to promote will prove to be more than mere 'paper' exercises, that they will in fact lead to changes in what pupils actually receive from the curriculum they are offered, and not only in the official statements in which that curriculum is expressed. It is also intended to assist those who may be required to implement changes which are not of their own making – or choosing.

The overview it seeks to provide is also aimed at assisting in the process of raising the level of professional understanding of change and the curriculum. For a properly professional understanding is always important, but it becomes particularly important when changes in the curriculum are being brought about by those who lack this depth of understanding and who see the process of educational change in simple terms, as something which can be readily achieved by acts of legislation, by the application of sanctions and by the distribution of myriad forms of documentation.

It is self-evident that the concern will also be to demonstrate that those who seek to change the school curriculum without regard to the knowledge, the insights and the understandings which have been derived from earlier experience, and without due regard for the necessity of adopting the appropriate strategies and mechanisms for achieving their goals, are likely to find that the changes they actually bring about are very different from those their planning envisaged, and, indeed, that the effects of their efforts are unlikely to lead to the improvements they are seeking and may well be detrimental to the quality of educational provision.

In Chapter 1 we explore the concept of change, consider the different responses which have been made to the phenomenon of change, and look at the implications of those different responses for educational planning and for the notion of curriculum change.

In Chapter 2 we introduce the theoretical perspectives which have emerged from a number of studies of the practice of curriculum change; attempts which have been made to create a conceptual framework for analysing and understanding the processes of educational change.

Based on the theoretical discussions of these first two chapters, Chapters 3 and 4 undertake a review of some of the attempts which have been made to change the school curriculum. Chapter 3 considers attempts which have been made to do this on a national scale and the impact on the curriculum, the changes brought about almost unconsciously, which have resulted from other kinds of national initiative. Chapter 4 looks critically at the notion of school-based or school-centred initiatives in order to identify how far and in what ways such initiatives can lead to effective and lasting forms of curriculum change. Chapter 5 examines the use of rhetoric to effect change, and the language of educational discourse.

# 1

# THE CONCEPT OF CHANGE

Why *should* we change the school curriculum? Or why should we strive to create the conditions under which it can change? These are perfectly reasonable and legitimate questions from which to start our exploration of curriculum change. There have been many theorists of education, from Plato onwards, who have held a concept of education which has entailed a view of the curriculum as a fixed and static entity, as the only device for bringing about the desired educational processes. Such views have often been reflected in educational practices. One has only to think of the vigour with which, until relatively recently, the study of classics was extolled and propounded as the only route to a 'proper' education, and the reluctance that was displayed, especially in the private sector of education, to allow the classical curriculum to become diluted by the addition of such 'utilitarian' subjects as science and modern languages. We have in the National Curriculum a current example of a fixed and static curriculum, with built-in devices to ensure permanence rather than to permit or promote change.

The question of why we should seek to change the curriculum or to permit it to change is thus one that must be faced. And it is an issue that requires – logically – to be explored first, before we begin to examine theoretical analyses of curriculum change or the mechanics and the strategies of curriculum change.

This opening chapter seeks to erect a theoretical backcloth against which subsequent chapters will consider the realities of changing the school curriculum and of creating a framework which may allow such change to occur continuously, and which will provide the necessary theoretical and intellectual perspective from which such issues must be examined.

In so doing the chapter will argue for the importance of change and the necessity of devising a curriculum framework which not only permits but also encourages it. For its general theme will be that change must be recognized as an ever-present phenomenon of life and that any aspect of human existence, and especially of social living, which is planned without reference to that fact is fated to be ineffectual and to inhibit rather than to promote the quality of that existence.

# THE CONCEPT OF CHANGE

For as long as we are aware that human beings have philosophized about the world and about human existence, in both the Western and the Eastern traditions, concern has continually been expressed about the ever-changing nature of all things, about the impermanence of all aspects of the world as we know it. In the Western tradition it was the consciousness of this impermanence that was the genesis of Western philosophy, since what the early Ionian philosophers were engaged in was a search for some underlying permanence, some stability in the face of the uncertainty of all physical – and human – phenomena. This uncertainty was expressed by one of the leading figures in that tradition, Heracleitus, in the assertion that 'everything is in a state of flux', and, more graphically, 'you cannot step twice into the same river'. Aristotle was later to make the same point when he said 'All things are in motion; nothing steadfastly is'.

Initially the focus was on the physical world; the exploration was as much scientific (although not in the sense of involving empirical enquiry) as it was philosophical. And the concern was with understanding that physical world, the world of 'phenomena', with how we can generate any real knowledge of such a changing and shifting entity. Inevitably, however, and very quickly, the focus extended to include social phenomena, changes in human relationships, in human and social values and in social systems, so that, as we shall see, important political implications began to emerge and the concept of change was seen as applying to social change as well as to changes in the physical world.

The first response to this awareness of change was to seek for some underlying permanence, some unchanging entity or rule or law which would, as it were, override the change itself and offer a basis for some kind of certain knowledge. For Heracleitus himself this was the notion of universal reason, the 'logos' ('the word' of St John's Gospel), God, a 'conception of unity in diversity' (Copleston, 1966, p. 40).

Change and decay in all around I see.
O Thou who changest not . . .

For a contemporary of Heracleitus, Anaxagoras, it was 'nous' (mind), and, although he expressed this theory in a mystical and embryonic form only (using Mind, as Aristotle later said, as a *deus ex machina* to solve every problem), this notion that in some sense it is the mind, or reason, or rationality, which imposes permanence and order on the ever-changing phenomena of existence, became the basic premise of that rationalist epistemology which dominated Western philosophy for more than 2,000 years – and is still in evidence (although no longer unchallenged).

Thus Plato saw 'true' knowledge as that generated by the mind or the intellect, in contrast to that inferior form of 'belief' or 'opinion' which is all that the evidence of our senses can offer. And he saw all knowledge as one, as potentially perfect and as held together by the coping stone of the supreme 'Form of Beauty, Truth and Goodness' (a concept which, it must be noted, brings together the physical and the human or social, and thus extends the concept of certain and perfect knowledge far beyond the confines of scientific knowledge and into that of morals, aesthetics and even politics). Augustine, Aquinas and all the Christian philosophers saw the source of such perfect knowledge as God, the supreme, all-knowing being. For Kant and the other German Idealists, it was rationality, the source of knowledge which is perfect, true and certain, in contrast to the imperfect, un-certain and shifting nature of that which we apprehend only through our senses and our sense-experience.

Thus there has been within philosophy an almost universal accept-ance of the power of mind, of reason, of rationality, with or without the help of God, to identify the certainties which, it has been believed, must lie behind the apparent uncertainties of human experience of both natural and human phenomena. As a result claims have been made, and continue to be made, not only for the validity of scientific and mathematical 'truths' but also for the validity of assertions made in the aesthetic, the moral and the political fields too. Reason, or rationality, has been seen not only as enabling us to generate certain knowledge of the physical world but also as the source of *indisputable* 'truths' in the area of social, moral and political life. Beauty, it is claimed, is an objective notion, not a matter of opinion; morality is also similarly objective; and that leads ultimately, and inevitably, to claims for objectively perfect forms of political structures and social systems. Thus Spinoza could write his *Ethics* in the form of mathematical theorems in the style of Euclid. Kant could offer us theories of morals and of aesthetics making similar claims to certainty. And Hegel could set up a rationalist political theory which, offering as it did a view of political structures evolving towards some kind of ultimate perfection, provided, at least in part, the theoretical basis and philosophical underpinning for fascism, and, albeit by a slightly different route, for Marxism.

Furthermore, it will be clear that this kind of acceptance of the notion of objective 'truths' in all fields entails a commitment also to a concept of 'perfection'. For it requires us to accept that perfect knowledge is possible in every dimension of human experience, since it is only from some such source as this that we can acquire the objective criteria against which to demonstrate the validity of these indisputable 'truths'. If we are to be able to claim the status of timeless and unquestionable validity for any 'truth' in any sphere, we must do so by reference to the yardstick of what constitutes perfection in that sphere. That which makes a work of art a manifestation of some aesthetic 'truth' must be the fact that it reflects, at least to a significant degree, perfect beauty. That which makes a moral act objectively and indisputably good is that it reflects perfect morality. And what makes a political system 'right' is that it reflects the perfect form of political organization.

This kind of view cannot stand without the foundation of some notion of perfection. Such a notion must be mystical and metaphysical in nature, since not even the most dedicated rationalist would wish to claim that we have had empirical evidence of perfection in any sphere. Indeed, the essence of rationalist epistemology is that we can only achieve these kinds of understanding by going beyond our empirical observations. Thus the concept of 'perfection' is essentially a priori, independent of experience; indeed, it transcends experience; it is thus literally metaphysical. As such, for some people, it lacks conviction when offered as the basis not only for a theory of knowledge but also for a theory of existence, a theory of how we should conduct ourselves – aesthetically, morally and politically.

The challenge to this view came with the emergence of an alternative epistemological theory, that known as empiricism, whose major claim, as the name suggests, is that the human mind cannot of itself create knowledge a priori, and that all we can claim to know is that which we have apprehended through our senses. As John Locke put it, 'no knowledge enters the mind except through the gates of the senses', the mind at birth is 'white paper, void of all characters, without any ideas', and 'I see no reason therefore to believe that the soul thinks before the senses have furnished it with ideas to think on'.

These ideas with which the senses furnish the mind, however, are exactly those uncertain, ever-changing phenomena of the world, both physical and human, which the rationalists had been claiming cannot be the source of anything worthy of being called 'knowledge'. Indeed, the next major exponent of empiricism, David Hume, was to accept and assert exactly that. The world is constantly changing; there is no source from which we can acquire any form of certainty or permanence with which to impose order on this constant state of flux. In Hume's view there is no secure basis for knowledge of any kind – scientific or aesthetic/moral/social/political.

This kind of view offered a healthy counterblast to the certainties of rationalism. However, it did so at a cost. Although it might be argued that the basis for the advance of knowledge which rationalism seemed to offer creates its own difficulties, it has to be recognized that the alternative, which seemed to be asserting that no kind of knowledge at all is possible, was perhaps even less satisfactory. It had the merit of protecting us from dogma in the fields of aesthetics and morals and politics, but only by undermining at the same time all our developing scientific knowledge and understanding.

It was this that first prompted Kant to resurrect a rationalist epistemology, based on a detailed critique of knowledge, but this led him too, as we have seen, to attempt to claim similar certainties in the realms of morals and aesthetics; and it led Hegel subsequently to offer a political theory whose major tenet was that the state is the embodiment of reason and thus not to be challenged by the individual – a metaphysical theory of the state which probably did more to discredit this form of rationalist epistemology than any other feature of it. It has to be recognized, however, that any attempt to understand the world as embodying rationality in some form such as this – the 'logos', universal reason, God – must ultimately lead to this kind of view of society and of social living, and must elevate the collective, whether the state or any other social grouping, above the individual. These are the inevitable effects of attempting to impose permanence in this way on the ever-changing phenomena of the world and of human existence.

There was thus a reaction against Hegel's philosophy, not least through the work of those philosophers who have come, somewhat misleadingly, to be given the collective title of 'existentialists'. The movement against theories of permanence was also accelerated by the work of Charles Darwin, his view of continuous evolution becoming a major theme of intellectual activity in all fields in the second half of the nineteenth century.

Thus, by the beginning of the present century there had been a major rethinking in this area. The great intellectual message of this century has been that which was put rather crudely by Nietzsche in the assertion that 'God is dead'. What Nietzsche was claiming was that rationalism had had its day, that metaphysical philosophy had had its day, that certainty of knowledge had had its day, and that we must learn to live with the realities of evolution and change, and to cope with the uncertainties they create.

Thus the present century has seen the collapse of several forms of totalitarian political system, since these have been based on an assumed and spurious concept of moral and political 'truths' and certainty, and have consequently not been able to respond to inevitable social and political change. It has seen an erosion of the concept of 'truth' in all fields of intellectual endeavour, including those of mathematics and science. This development, far from slowing down the rate of technological progress, has had the opposite effect and has opened up the way to massive technological advance, a 'knowledge explosion', since it has encouraged challenge to the status quo and a constant questioning of it. At the same time it has offered a perfectly sound working model of knowledge as axiomatic or hypothetical and thus as tentative, temporary and subject to continuous change, evolution and development. Change has thus been accepted and a theory of knowledge developed which can accommodate it. In art too, this century has seen major changes, again attributable to the offering of challenges to traditional forms and styles. There has been 'a revolution in philosophy', as philosophers have shifted the focus of their attentions from a search for 'eternal truths', or for some ultimate and all-embracing solution to the problems of knowledge and existence, to the much more mundane, but much more helpful and productive, attempt to analyse the concepts used in all areas of enquiry in order to facilitate their advance, to the development of techniques of enquiry rather than the offering of indisputable prescriptions, and from a rationalist to an empiricist epistemology. In most areas of the social sciences too, positivism has given way to approaches which reflect more limited, but more intellectually honest forms of endeavour, attempts to understand and perhaps to explain social phenomena rather than to offer eternal prescriptions for social and political living. In all of these fields the Platonic search after certainty has been replaced by a Socratic form of constant questioning. Change has been regarded not as an illusion, as unreal or unsatisfactory, nor as something to be explained away and concealed behind some theory of permanence. Rather it has been recognized, and even embraced, as an essential part of the world and of the human condition and as the source of that which gives value to individual human existence.

And so, in the latter part of the twentieth century, humankind has seen substantial shifts in the way in which the world is known and experienced – shifts from Newtonian to quantum science, from modernist to post-modernist cultural forms and from Fordism to flexible accumulation as the dominant mode of economic production. Indeed, a number of writers from diverse fields of intellectual enquiry have interpreted these shifts as manifestations of a more substantial shift from modernity to post-modernity. But we have been slow to recognize that shift, and its implications, in the social sciences and especially in education.

Thus, as William E. Doll (1989, p. 243) expresses it, 'we see our vision of the universe turning from the simple, stable one of Newtonian modernism to the complex, chaotic, finite one of post-modernism'. And that vision extends to all areas of human thought and understanding. The Newtonian paradigm has been abandoned in our search for greater understanding in the scientific and mathematical fields. It has persisted, however, in the social sciences and in educa-tion. Doll's concern is to argue that it has 'radical implications for education and curriculum' (ibid.) and to persuade us to begin to seek after a 'post-modern' analysis of those implications. We will return to this later when we explore ways in which theories of education have responded to the phenomenon of change.

We can thus see that there have been several different responses to that phenomenon, and it will be worth our while briefly to identify these, since they will all be seen to have relevance to the question with which we began – why should we change the school curriculum or strive to create the conditions under which it can change?

## RESPONSE TO THE NOTION OF CHANGE

It will be clear from what has been said already that thinkers – and non-thinkers too – have adopted a number of different attitudes towards the notion of change and have responded in several different ways to the recognition that all aspects of the world and of human existence are far from static.

For some, change – and especially social change – has been viewed as a process of deterioration from some kind of golden age of perfection; change is the process by which things get worse rather than better. One does not have to look far to find this kind of pessimistic view in the attitudes of people in respect of many aspects of life – sporting and artistic as well as moral and political. At the level of serious and careful philosophical speculation too this phenomenon can be readily recognized. The response to this view of change is to attempt to arrest it, to stop things from getting worse, to keep things as they are, or, better, to take them back to where they used to be.

In politics, whatever its theoretical underpinning, this is the essence of totalitarianism. Plato saw the evolution of political systems towards what he regarded as the inferior system of democracy as evidence of such deterioration, and recommended the establishment of a political system whose purpose (to be achieved, it is worth noting, largely through the system of education) was to arrest this process and maintain the status quo. And there is a sense in which the etymology of the term 'conservatism' implies a similar view. The first major attempt to produce a rationale for conservative politics – and not many such are to be seen – was that of Edmund Burke, who, sharing the alarm felt by many at the changes being brought about in revolutionary Europe, and especially by the excesses of the French revolution, propounded a political philosophy whose essence was the belief that, whatever inadequacies are to be found in existing forms of government, they are unlikely to be as bad as those that will attend any new form of government we may erect to replace them. Burke, it must be acknowledged, was not offering here some metaphysical notion of change as deterioration from an age of perfection, merely the eminently practical wisdom of one who felt that evolution was preferable to revolution. Fundamentally, however, his view is that change is to be resisted, or at least decelerated, and it is this that renders his philosophy essentially 'conservative'.

This tendency to maintain the 'stable state' (Schon, 1971), whether or not based on a theory of change as deterioration, is a recognizable feature of human nature, and is worth noting here since we will need to return to it in our later explorations of the realities of curriculum change and innovation in schools. It is characterized by what Schon (1971) has termed 'dynamic conservatism', that tendency of individuals and of organizations to strive to maintain the status quo. Thus innovations are resisted by every possible device to ensure that they do not 'take'. They are ignored, opposed, isolated, redirected, subjected to whatever response seems most likely to kill them off or deflect them from their intended purpose of altering the circumstances under which we conduct our professional lives and the professional tasks we face.

It is worth noting finally that the view of change as deterioration, as leading to social and political structures essentially inferior to those they replace, only makes sense in a context of some accepted notion of objective and unchallengeable moral and political values, and, consequently, of some notion of 'perfection'. One can only make claims about 'better' or 'worse', about 'deterioration', against some kind of criterion or standard of what is objectively 'good' or 'perfect'. Such a view thus reflects, whether consciously and overtly or not, a rationalist epistemology of the kind we saw earlier attempts to offer credence to and a justification of, the concept of objective moral, social and political standards.

The second kind of intellectual response to a recognition of the notion of change also accepts this rationalist view of the objectivity of moral, social and political values, and with it a concept of perfection. This view, however, sees change as leading us not away from a perfect state, but towards it.

Many of those who have, as we saw earlier, posited some kind of underlying rationale to the uncertainties and the impermanence of the world, both physical and social and political, have gone beyond the recognition of the imperfections of present existence, and even beyond the assumption of some underlying permanence which will explain them, and have claimed that what we are experiencing here and now is but a stage in an inevitable and inexorable process of development towards some ultimately perfect state. Some notion such as this may lie behind the religious belief in another world, a perfect life hereafter, a world to be contrasted with the imperfect world in which we live.

A much more carefully argued view of this kind of inevitable progress towards ultimate perfection is to be found in the philosophy of Hegel. As we saw earlier, Hegel took Kant's notion that there is an underlying rationality to all aspects of existence and developed it into a form of idealism which is idealist in every sense – not only in the sense of assuming a greater permanence and reality for the 'ideas' of things than that enjoyed by their practical or empirical manifestations, but also in the sense of assuming that all is progress towards an ideal, a form of perfection.

For Hegel, rationality itself develops and proceeds by a triadic process of dialectic. Every experience, assertion, piece of knowledge is to be seen as a *thesis* which will ultimately come face to face with its *antithesis*, a contradiction, a phenomenon or set of phenomena which do not fit or match its claims, which are not compatible with it. The result of this clash is some kind of *synthesis*, as the new phenomena are assimilated into the old. This synthesis in turn becomes a new thesis, the process repeating itself perpetually as knowledge continues to develop. Ultimately, through this continuous process perfect knowledge will be achieved. This Hegel called the 'Absolute'; and it can be seen as a more sophisticated version of that Platonic view of knowledge we noted earlier – knowledge as complete, whole, perfect and held together by the ultimate Form of Beauty, Truth and Goodness.

As a characterization of how knowledge and understanding develop – at least in the scientific field – this notion of a dialectical process is not unhelpful. Scientists do work within accepted scientific principles, until they encounter phenomena which cannot be explained or accommodated within those principles; the principles are then modified and adapted to allow for the new phenomena. Thus we may have a theory of flotation linked to the properties of materials until we note that, under certain conditions, materials with a specific gravity greater than that of water will float in water; we then modify our theory to take account of displacement.

The claim that this process is leading to ultimate perfection of knowledge, however, is more difficult to accept; and the application of this schema to human development – moral, social and political – raises even greater difficulties. For Hegel it led to an acceptance of war as the dialectical conflict between nations and an inevitable part of the process of political development towards the 'Absolute', to that metaphysical theory of the state and of the individual's inferior role within it which we noted earlier, to a dialectic of history which saw every historical event as a manifestation of the 'Absolute' or the 'World Spirit' and, therefore not subject to any kind of moral appraisal. 'Whatever is, is right because it is.' 'Reason dominates the world and world history is thus a natural process.' 'World history . . . is the world's court of judgement.'

Karl Marx's development of this theory exhibits the same difficulties. Marx's historical dialectic is a materialist rather than a metaphysical dialectic. The conflict is between classes rather than between nations. But it makes the same assumptions about the processes of history leading inexorably to an ultimate state of perfection – the proletarian dictatorship and the end of the state, the classless and stateless society, when, as Engels said, 'the state is not abolished. It dies out'. Again, therefore, we see that change is conceived as an inevitable process, over which we have no direct control, and which is leading to an ultimate form of perfection – this time social and political perfection as well as a perfect, complete and whole edifice of knowledge.

On this view, if our current knowledge can be seen as imperfect, that is because it is only a stage in the process of development which is taking us to perfection of knowledge, to Plato's 'Form of Beauty, Truth and Goodness', to Hegel's 'Absolute'. If our moral understanding is similarly imperfect, again that is because we have not yet reached moral perfection. If our political structures leave much to be desired, that is because we are still well short of the perfect political system, of Marx's 'stateless society', for example. The essence of this view, however, is that 'it will all be right on the night'; it will all come together in the end.

Thus change is seen as 'development', in the strong sense of that term, as movement towards that which is better than what we have at the present, and ultimately to that which is best or perfect. This view of change as development is a very common view. We must, however, recognize that it is merely one of many views one can take of change.

The main difficulty with this view of change as explicable in terms of some underlying rational process of inevitable development (apart from its mysticism, its metaphysical base and its highly problematic assumptions about the nature, and, indeed, the existence, of a concept of perfection) is the implications it has for the freedom of the individual. We noted earlier that for Hegel the state and its demands must always take precedence over the interests of the individual. For him the state is in some way the realization of individual freedom. 'In duty the individual finds his liberation' and World Spirit is 'above the point of view from which the fortunes of individuals matter'. The interests of individuals are subjective interests and thus not to be regarded as enjoying the same status as the objective demands of the state as the embodiment of reason.

Marxism too denies individual freedom and diversity. The progress of human society and relationships will come about not through the efforts of individuals but through the inevitable process by which the dialectic works itself out in history. And the final stage of ultimate perfection can only be perfect if individuals do not exercise any kind of individuality or freedom but accept their role in the collective of the classless, stateless society.

Any such view of change as the manifestation of some underlying permanence must elevate the collective above the individual, the universal above the particular, the rational above the human, in the way that these theories do. In denying individualism it must also deny freedom. For, if people are to exercise their freedom, they will do so by challenging the universal, especially in the fields of aesthetics, morals and politics, by expressing their individual views on issues of beauty and goodness, especially as these might be reflected in political structures. In doing so the individual is denying this view of a permanence underlying change, rejecting the concept of perfection which underpins this view and offering a challenge to the rationalist epistemology which is at the root of this kind of philosophical position.

Hegel and Marx have been seen, along with Plato, as 'the enemies of the open society' (Popper, 1945) precisely because their views, by elevating the collective, the universal, deny the freedom of the individual and support the notion of the 'closed' society, the society which is structured in such a way as to maintain the status quo or to permit change only in those directions which are regarded as historically determined, the kind of society we would describe as totalitarian, the arrested state. It is not just the freedom of the individual that is at stake here, therefore, it is also the whole issue of the nature of society and the existence of what one might wish to call a free society.

A commitment to the idea of a free and open society requires that we adopt a different view of the phenomenon of change. And it is to this third kind of response that we now turn.

For the third response to the recognition of change, a response which has typified most areas of human enquiry in the twentieth century, is to accept the fact of change, without seeking for any broad metaphysical interpretations to underscore it and without positing any concept of perfection – of knowledge, of values, of aesthetics, of morals, of political systems, of anything – towards or from which this change is taking us.

A major influence on the intellectual climate of the twentieth century has been the work of Charles Darwin and its central concept of the evolution of species. This work has influenced thinking in many areas and in many ways. What is relevant here is that it has highlighted the fact of constant change, of evolution, and has gone further and explained this change and evolution in scientific/empirical terms rather than by appealing to mystical and metaphysical concepts. It has explained change in terms of adaptation to a constantly changing environment and not in relation to any concept of ultimate perfection.

Darwin's concern was with biological and genetic evolution, but the influence of his work has spread far beyond those confines. Through the work of people such as John Dewey, for example, it has been given philosophical and sociological dimensions. Dewey has argued for an acceptance of the concept of evolution in all areas. We must accept, he claims, that knowledge is constantly evolving, that values are similarly evolving and that societies are evolving too; that nothing in human nature or relationships can be properly or usefully viewed as static and that to treat anything as such will lead to disaster, or, at the very least, will result in a slowing down of the evolutionary process. In short, we need not to arrest change, nor to accelerate it, but rather to facilitate it, to be constantly responsive to it, to learn to live with it. We thus have what we might call a sociology as well as a philosophy of change.

This view is closely linked to that shift from a rationalist to an empiricist epistemology which we noted earlier. It entails a rejection of any notion of perfection, of any idea of an underlying rationale, whether this be God or rationality, whether it be mystical or metaphysical, and of any concept of ultimate, objective, unquestionable values in any field. It entails an acceptance of the fact that all knowledge is tentative and hypothetical, open to challenge and debate in order to be responsive to continued evolution and development, and that this is especially true in the field of human values – aesthetic, moral, social and political.

In short, it cannot see change as development, but only as change. Certainly, change in scientific and technological knowledge leads to what we rightly call 'advance'; it plainly represents an improvement on what was there before, on the knowledge it 'replaces' or 'develops'. This view does not, however, claim that this is a process towards some metaphysical concept of complete and perfect knowledge – even in the scientific sphere. As a result it encourages us to view human change – aesthetic, moral, social and political – in the same light: change is change. If it is useful and helpful, then it is to be accepted and appreciated; if not, then not. For it must be acknowledged that some change – especially in the human field – is not acceptable to all and is therefore not appreciated by all. It can thus be rejected by those who do not find it welcome. There are no grounds for forcing them to accept it as necessarily 'good for them' because it represents a stage in the process of development towards a condition of perfection. Change is thus not necessarily development. And the two concepts need to be clearly distinguished, perhaps especially in the context of educational change. Alternatively, we should be careful to use the term 'development' in a purely neutral and descriptive sense, or perhaps, further, as suggesting nothing more than a process of smooth transition from one form to another, but not entailing commitment to some rationalist concept of perfection.

We return here to the claims made by Doll (1989). For it is to this 'post-modern' view of change that he is pointing us, a view of change as 'transformatory' as opposed to accumulative or incremental.

Such a view of change requires that we create and maintain the social conditions and context in which such continuous evolution can occur. If we see change from this perspective, if we recognize that knowledge and values must be allowed to evolve and human institutions must be permitted to 'develop' in phase with them, then we must have a social and political climate in which this can happen. It was for this reason that John Dewey advocated democratic forms of social living, not in support of any one such form, but to promote the continued existence of societies open to such continuous change, 'development', evolution. It was for this reason too that he advocated a democratic form of education which would be responsive to such changes and ensure the production of citizens who were similarly responsive.

An acceptance of a view of change such as this has accelerated many of those dramatic 'developments' of the twentieth century – social, moral and political as well as scientific and technological – which we noted earlier. Finally, there are two aspects of this view that we should note.

First, it is a view that reinstates those notions of individuality and freedom which we saw other theories fundamentally deny. Not only does it invite challenge to all forms of 'accepted wisdom', it further regards such challenge as essential to continued 'development' in all fields.

Second, it is not only in the fields of mathematics, science and technology that such a view of change and evolution has had the effect of unleashing the forces of dramatic change. It has had the same effect also in relation to human values as expressed in art, in aesthetics, in morals and in politics. It thus necessitates not only that there be freedom to challenge what might be seen as currently accepted knowledge in areas which may be seen as largely scientific and empirical, it also requires that there be freedom to challenge what might be pressed upon us as 'accepted' forms in art, in aesthetics, in morals and in social and political life. In short, it is a view of change which is incompatible with the existence of restrictions on freedom of thought and expression.

There are important implications for educational change and practice in such a view, which we will examine later.

First, however, we must explore more fully the links between technological change and social change. For it is not merely that both occur. They are in many ways interlinked and their interlinkings we must now consider.

## TECHNOLOGICAL CHANGE AND SOCIAL CHANGE

Technological change, largely because of its very rapidity, has received a good deal of attention in all quarters in recent years. One remembers Prime Minister Harold Wilson's reference to the 'white heat' of technological change, and the development of all societies over the last several decades has reflected the attempt to cope with and respond to such change in all areas.

It is worth reminding ourselves that in education the initial impetus and motivation towards planned curriculum change came as a direct result of the launching by the USSR in 1957 of the space satellite, Sputnik I, and the need that was felt immediately in the Western world to ensure – through appropriate forms of educational provision as well as by other means – that we did not fall behind in technological developments, and especially in the space race. Most, if not all, of the changes in the school curriculum which subsequent years have witnessed, certainly those prompted by political initiatives, and especially the introduction of the National Curriculum in England and Wales, can only be understood by reference to the need felt to ensure that schooling should respond appropriately to these developments. Thus we have seen the advancement of technological subjects from their low status in the hierarchy of school subjects to fourth place in the National Curriculum league table. And we are seeing their extension into the primary curriculum too. Allied to this, we have also witnessed the growth of 'primary science', a development which, while being promoted and justified by many on purer educational grounds, can nevertheless best be understood as part of this curriculum response to technological advance.

One can of course dispute, or at least debate, the appropriateness of developing the curriculum in this way to meet and to match technological advance. For it is perfectly tenable to argue that the focus of educational provision should lie elsewhere than in an instrumental and utilitarian response to changing economic needs. On the other hand, it is not necessary for such response to be totally instrumental and utilitarian. It is difficult not to accept that the curriculum should be planned, at least in part, to help young people to learn to live in the society into which they have been born. When that society is one which is characterized by rapid technological change, that means preparing them to live in a rapidly changing society.

Such preparation, however, involves far more than making them technologically skilled and aware. For technological change inevitably brings with it social, moral and, often, political change too. It leads to changes in our value systems as well as in the material circumstances of our lives. Evolution involves continuous adaptation to a constantly changing environment. In the case of human evolution this process of adaptation to the environment is, in its most obvious manifestations, technological development. For 'the basic premise of design and technological activity is that, using materials, tools and systems, human beings can intervene to modify and improve their environment' (DES/APU, 1987 p. 8). It is fallacious, however, to assume that this process can go on within, and have reference to, the physical environment alone. The human environment has many dimensions, and changes cannot occur in one without there being repercussions in the others. There can be no technological or scientific development which does not raise problems of a moral kind, and our response to those moral problems will bring about changes to our value systems which are as significant as the changes in the physical environment which prompted them, even though neither these moral changes nor their full significance may be as clearly recognized.

Thus, if scientific advance offers us the power to transplant organs from one body to another, it also presents us with the moral problem of deciding whether to use this power and under what conditions and in what circumstances we will regard its use as being acceptable or permissible. Our response to these questions will dramatically alter the moral context of our lives at several levels. At the individual level it will affect how one conducts one's own life and how one reacts individually to the culture of one's society. At the level of society itself it will lead to changes in the social mores, as we can appreciate by considering, for example, the changes in sexual mores which have followed the scientific developments in methods of birth control, including abortion. And at the political level it may ultimately lead to major structural changes, as we can see from the progressive democratization of societies. Perhaps the most influential factor here is the advance in communications technology which has led not only to the more efficient and more rapid dissemination of ideas and information but also to a greater awareness of issues and a more coherent and immediate response to them. There is no doubt that it is the inexorable movement of technological developments of this kind that has led, for example, to the erosion of Marxist–Leninist forms of totalitarian government in what was once known as the Eastern bloc.

If education is to respond in some way, therefore, to technological change, it must at the same time respond to the moral, social and political change which is an integral part of it. And those questions we raised earlier about the forms, the nature, the suitability of the educational response must not be addressed without a full awareness of the central importance of this dimension of the problem. To contemplate and plan curriculum change as a response merely to the technological aspects of human evolution is to misconceive the nature of that evolution and to lose sight of the essential role of values within it. It is thus to fail to produce a curriculum which addresses technological change in anything more sophisticated or substantial than an instrumental, utilitarian and economic context.

We have identified the phenomenon of cultural change. If culture is defined as comprising all aspects of the life of a society or of any group of people – its customs, its ways of life, its beliefs, its attitudes, its art, its social mores – then the kinds of change we are describing here are cultural changes. We noted earlier that those changes which the present century has witnessed have included changes in attitudes to and views of art, philosophy and religion as well as technology, morals and politics. There has been a cultural revolution. To some extent these changes derive from technological advance. But we must note that they are also attributable to that same change in our concept of knowledge which we have claimed has promoted that technological advance itself. Cultural change is to a large extent the product of an acceptance that cultural values – aesthetic, moral, political, and even religious – are not fixed and absolute. They are there to be challenged – and changed. The opposite view, that such cultural values are in some sense eternal and indisputable, has been challenged in this way and rejected. It has been seen to be a primitive and untenable view of culture and represents an unjustifiable claim to the superiority of one culture over others. 'He is a barbarian, and thinks that the customs of his tribe and island are the laws of nature' (G. B. Shaw, *Caesar and Cleopatra*).

This last point draws our attention also to the fact of cultural diversity. The view that cultural diversity is not only to be recognized but also accepted is slowly gaining ground. We are less likely nowadays, for example, to claim superiority for Western classical music over what used to be regarded as 'decadent' (note the 'golden age' view of change) black jazz. We are in fact in general interested in and admiring of all forms of art, whatever their origin. And we are in general less inclined to assume that our way of life is in some indefinable way more 'advanced' than that of other nations. Many may still assume such positions of extreme jingoism, but hardly anyone would be prepared to attempt to make out an intellectual case for these positions.

Thus a recognition of social and cultural change must bring with it a recognition and an acceptance of cultural diversity. This is only the case, however, against a concept of change as fact rather than change as value, and, just as we saw earlier that there are several responses one can make to the phenomenon of change itself, so there are several different ways in which education and the school curriculum can respond to such changes in society. It will be helpful if we now consider some of these.

## EDUCATION AND CHANGE

It was suggested in the last section that the notion of evolution makes continuous change of both a technological and a social kind inevitable. Education must allow for this, it must respond to it in some way, and it must be planned in such a way as to permit it to allow for and to respond to change. Its response will of course depend on the view of change upon which it is predicated, and different views of change will give rise to different notions about how education and the curriculum should be planned to respond to it.

Thus, those who view change as some kind of deterioration from a golden age of perfection will wish to arrest it. This was the attitude taken by the contributors to those Black Papers (Cox and Dyson, 1969a, 1969b; Cox and Boyson, 1977), which, when curriculum change began to occur in the 1960s and 1970s in the United Kingdom, inveighed against it as, almost by definition, reflecting a lowering of standards. Their attitude to social and technological change was never made clear, but to acknowledge change in society and to resist it in education is a very odd position to adopt intellectually. Nevertheless, in those publications, and in others like them, we can see one response to curriculum change – arrest it, since it must be for the worse. It would of course be argued by the authors of these publications that it was certain particular kinds of change rather than change *per se* about which they were expressing concern. However, nowhere do their own recommendations go beyond maintaining the status quo.

It is perhaps equally unsatisfactory, on the other hand, to regard change as being necessarily for the better, as progress towards some form of nirvana, some ultimate state of educational perfection, since, as we saw earlier, the very concept of perfection is a difficult one to espouse. Some approaches to educational change and innovation, however, have been based on this kind of assumption – again whether well thought through or not is another question. At the micro level, in order to recognize this, we need do no more than note the bland assumptions which have sometimes been made about school-based forms of curriculum development, which, as we shall see when we consider these in more detail in Chapter 4, have often been regarded as unquestionably for the better. At the macro level, the best example of this attitude must be those views of 'progressive' education, such as were outlined in the Plowden Report (CACE, 1967), which, by the very meaning of the term used to describe them, have been assumed to be leading inevitably to 'progress', towards something better – a notion which again is meaningless without appeal to some concept of perfection, a concept which philosophically and logically is incompatible with what these theories have wanted to say about the fundamentals of the educational process. As we saw with the more esoteric philosophical responses to change, both of these views suffer from the same kinds of deficiency, since both appeal to some metaphysical system of ultimate, and perfect, values.

The third kind of response to change we noted earlier is that which accepts it as nothing more than a fact of human existence, as an inevitable feature of the world we inhabit. In the context of education this takes the form of accepting change as a given and attempting to devise the most appropriate ways in which the school curriculum can respond to it, or as Doll (1989) suggests, recognizing it as trans-formatory rather than viewing it as accumulative or incremental. This is a view of change as 'associated with chaos, complexity, confusion and uncertainty' (op.cit., p. 249), and one in the light of which 'errors are seen as necessary actions in the process of development – the motors which drive development' (ibid.). It is not a view that is widely accepted in the educational debate, although 'theories of chaos, un-certainty and confusion [are] taking ever increasing roles in the fields of management, mathematics, political science, physics and sociology' (ibid.).

What might constitute appropriate forms of response in the context of this view of change? Clearly, it is not appropriate to ignore change or to try to arrest it, since this view begins from an acceptance of its inevitability. Nor is it appropriate to assume that, whatever form it takes, it must *ipso facto* be for the better. What kind of preparation do pupils need if they are to be educated satisfactorily and effectively in and for a changing society? What kind of approach to education, to knowledge and to learning is appropriate to such a changing society?

In answer to the first of those questions, it will be almost self-evident that, in preparation for a productive role in a changing society, young people need to be made aware of the fact of change and all its implications. They need to be discouraged from viewing anything, and especially the knowledge and values the school curriculum exposes them to, as fixed, permanent or unchallengeable. A curriculum which sees change as neither bad nor good but merely as a fact of life will set out to prepare pupils for the fact of continuous change. Such a curriculum will respond to technological change not by setting out a body of scientific and technological knowledge designed to meet that technological change which has already occurred, but by endeavouring to prepare pupils for the change that will go on occurring.

It is thirty years since the Crowther Report (CACE, 1959) raised for us the questions of 'education in a changing world' and advised that 'the first quality that is needed to cope with such a world is adaptability' (op.cit., p. 52). It went on to say that 'the need for adaptability exposes an ambiguity in the word "skill"' (ibid.) and, later, that 'it may be that there will even be a reduced need in the future for "skill" in the old-fashioned sense of the term; what will be needed in ever growing volume will be the quality that can perhaps best be described as "general mechanical intelligence"' (op.cit., p. 53). The experience we have had in the years which have followed the publication of that report, experience of the ever-increasing rapidity of technological change, has done a great deal to strengthen and under-line that argument.

Yet the lesson is still to be learned. It may be getting home in relation to technology itself, but it has had little impact beyond that (even though the Crowther Report's comments were made in the context of a clear recognition of the realities of social as well as technological change). There is little, for example, in the National Curriculum which reflects an awareness of this issue, even though it has been offered as a curriculum designed to 'develop the potential of all pupils and equip them for the responsibilities of citizenship and for the challenges of employment in *tomorrow's* world' (DES, 1987, p. 2, emphasis added).

This may explain why the attainment targets in Design and Technology within the National Curriculum, unlike those in most other subjects, are procedural rather than content based, stressing processes rather than content or products.

To limit this approach to Design and Technology, however, is not enough. If we were right in the previous section to argue that technological change must be conceived as going well beyond technology, then a curriculum to prepare pupils for the realities of change must seek to do so through its approach to all subjects, all its aspects and not just those entitled 'technology'. This suggests that we must look more closely at our approach to, our concept of, curriculum in all areas. We will return to this issue of curriculum change and concepts of curriculum in the next section.

First, however, we must briefly consider the second question which we suggested is raised for educational planners by an acceptance of change as fact rather than change as value: what kind of approach to educational planning at the macro level is appropriate and consonant with this acceptance?

We saw earlier that an acceptance of change as fact must lead us to a recognition of the need to create the conditions under which it can happen, and indeed flourish. The nature of the education a society provides is a very important aspect of those conditions. We have seen that the dramatic changes which this century, and especially its second half, have witnessed – in technology itself, but also in aesthetics, morals and politics – are largely attributable to a changed view of human knowledge. We have ceased to see knowledge in any sphere as fixed, static, God given, eternal, unchallengeable, unproblematic, and have begun to recognize it as fluid, tentative, hypothetical, necessarily open to constant questioning and highly problematic.

If continuing change is to be facilitated (and even the basic political desire for economic growth would seem to require this), then this view of knowledge must be promoted and embraced in all areas and at all levels. The acceptance of this view must begin in the schools; the curriculum must be planned to demonstrate this acknowledgement of the importance of flexibility and lack of dogmatism in the face of knowledge. Flexibility in our approach to knowledge must complement that adaptability we claimed is crucial in the development of the individual.

To say this is to do little more than to repeat the central message of the work of John Dewey, whose concept of democracy sprang from his commitment to the need to create the social and intellectual conditions under which continuous change and evolution could flourish – in the material conditions of our lives and in their aesthetic, social, moral and political dimensions too. Fundamental to this view is the claim that knowledge itself must be permitted to evolve. And that implies that we must take a new and quite different view of the role of knowledge in the school curriculum, as Dewey was at pains to point out. A truly democratic curriculum must do more than merely prepare pupils for life in a democratic society, for the 'responsibilities of citizenship' (DES, 1987, p. 2) in such a society. A democratic curriculum, in Dewey's sense, must be open to the continuous evolution of knowledge and values; it must alert pupils to that continuous evolution; and it must invite challenge to whatever seems to be the prevailing orthodoxy in any sphere. For without such challenge there can be no advancement; thesis can only move to synthesis when faced by antithesis.

In plain terms, the acceptance of change, of evolution in knowledge and values must invalidate any curriculum which focuses on the transmission of what currently counts as knowledge in any sphere and stresses the largely passive assimilation of this knowledge by the pupil. A dynamic view of knowledge entails a dynamic view of curriculum.

We thus return to the issue of concepts of curriculum in relation to concepts of change. Both that adaptability of the individual to continuous change and the flexibility of knowledge which is complementary to it require not only that we adopt a different approach to knowledge itself but also, and consequently, that we reconceptualize our definition of and our approach to the curriculum.

## CONCEPTS OF CURRICULUM

It is not the intention here to outline in detail the several different concepts of curriculum and approaches to curriculum planning which have emerged from both theoretical and practical sources during the last two decades. These must be familiar to all students of education, even though they have clearly escaped the attention of the authors of the National Curriculum and of those many documents which have emanated from the Department of Education and Science and from Her Majesty's Inspectorate (HMI) in support of it.

In broad terms, three quite distinct concepts of curriculum and models of curriculum planning can be discerned both in the practice of teachers and in the theoretical perspectives which have been offered as a basis for that practice. One can view the curriculum as a body of knowledge-content and/or subjects, and education as the process by which these are transmitted or 'delivered' to pupils by the most effective methods that can be devised. Or one can see education in terms of its products, designed to achieve certain ends or aims, and the curriculum consisting of a statement of the step-by-step shorter-term objectives by which these aims are to be attained. Or, finally, one can see education as a process or a series of processes, and the curriculum as a statement of the procedural principles in the light of which teachers will seek to support and promote those processes.

In short, being educated can be conceived in terms of what one knows or must be brought to know, or in terms of what one has become or must be made or helped to become, or in terms of how one has developed or should be helped to develop. And the curriculum can be conceived in terms of its content, its products, or its processes. Curriculum planning can be seen as requiring the prestatement either of knowledge-content and subjects, or of aims and objectives, or of procedural principles. And the teacher's task can be viewed as either to transmit that knowledge, or to achieve those aims by way of the step-by-step objectives, or to promote the processes of educational development by constant reference to those underlying procedural principles.

Much debate has focused on these contrasting views of education, of curriculum and of the teacher's role. And, as we have just said, this is not the place to explore or continue that debate. What is important here is the stance that these contrasting views entail towards knowledge and its role in the educative process, and, in particular, the extent to which each of them leads to the creation of a context in which that evolution of knowledge we have claimed is crucial can continue.

When one considers these three models in the light of that question, it becomes quickly apparent that the first two do not and cannot support the continued evolution of knowledge, because they are essentially predicated on a view of knowledge as largely fixed and static, offering no built-in allowance for the dynamic of knowledge. The content model requires us to state in advance what knowledge our pupils are to be required by the curriculum to assimilate. There may be a parallel concern that they should also come to understand this knowledge, to demonstrate a mastery of it as a body of understanding and not merely as a collection of 'facts'. But there can be no requirement that they be encouraged to challenge its validity, for such challenge relates to the processes of learning, not its content.

The 'aims and objectives' model sometimes, in some usages, offers no more than a methodological device by which mastery of bodies of knowledge-content can be most effectively achieved, suggesting that, if the aim is mastery of '*x*', then '*x*' should be broken down into smaller, 'bite-sized' objectives, since 'the most common educational objective . . . is the acquisition of knowledge or information' (Bloom 1956, p. 28).

Where the aims are framed in terms other than content, it is often very difficult, and sometimes impossible, to detect the conceptual differences between an aim and an objective. A good example of this is the HMI 'Curriculum Matters' series of publications. All of these offer lists of the aims and objectives of the particular subject which is their concern, but none of them attempts to provide any distinguishing definitions, and most offer the kind of lists of each which make it impossible for the reader to detect what the distinction is. It is, for example, an *aim* of history teaching to enable pupils 'to develop a knowledge of chronology within which they can organize their understanding of the past' (DES, 1988a, p. 3) and an *objective* (by the age of 16) to 'have acquired a firm and clear chronological framework within which to place and relate new information' (op.cit., p. 5). It is an *aim* 'to understand . . . that historical explanation is provisional, always debatable and sometimes controversial' (op.cit., p. 3) and an *objective* (again by age 16) to 'be aware of varied and often conflicting interpretations of past events' (op.cit., p. 5).

When the model is used in a more clearly considered way than this, and is not simply directed at mastery of knowledge-content, the role of knowledge within it is merely as a means to the goal of achieving one's aims, as in practice it must be in the examples given above. For the objectives set out 'the *intended behavior* (emphasis added) of students' (Bloom *et al.*, 1956, p. 12), and the selection of content is made according to its potential effectiveness in achieving these aims; it is in the main the answer to the question 'What educational experiences can be provided that are likely to attain these purposes?' (Tyler, 1949, p. 1). Thus the purpose of education on this model becomes not the acquisition of predetermined bodies of knowledge-content but the achievement of certain prestated behavioural changes in the pupil or student by exposure to appropriate knowledge.

One can argue that this view of education as the modification of behaviour is, or can be, a highly restrictive approach and unlikely to lead either to adaptability on the part of the individual (even if that were to be the stated aim) or to an acceptance of the flexibility of knowledge, both of which we have seen are essential prerequisites for the promotion of continuous change, and indeed for the creation of a democratic curriculum. And this is true even of the most sophisticated versions of this model and the most complex sets of objectives, so long as they are viewed in this light – as devices for changing the behaviour of the individual in predetermined directions. It is that very notion of predetermination that vitiates any concept of individual adaptability or of flexibility of knowledge. For to predetermine or predecide anything, whether it be knowledge-content to be transmitted or behavioural changes (however sophisticated) to be brought about, is to preclude the possibility of change, development, evolution or even modification, not to mention negotiation and choice on the part of the pupil or student.

It is for this reason that Doll (1989) claims that the present curriculum is based on the Newtonian paradigm.

> Direct correlations can be made between Madeline Hunter's or Ralph Tyler's notions of an orderly curriculum with ends pre-set and Newton's idea of a stable universe with planets rotating around the sun in perfect harmony. . . . Disturbance is not viewed here as a key, necessary, or desirable ingredient. Connections can also be made between B. F. Skinner's or James Popham's view of expressing learning in discrete, quantifiable and linear units and Newton's approach to the calculus. Both are reductionist, assume the whole to be no more than the sum of the parts, and lead to a curriculum which is cumulative rather than transformative.
>
> (op.cit., p. 242)

It would appear that neither a content nor an 'aims and objectives' approach to the curriculum is compatible with an acceptance of the constant state of change of human knowledge and understanding, or with a 'post-modern' view of change. And this is one reason why the alternative of the process model has emerged. It has come, at least in part, from a rejection of rationalist epistemology (Blenkin and Kelly, 1981, 1987a; Kelly, 1986, 1989), along with the confidence and certainty about human knowledge that such an epistemology offers, and an acceptance that in all things, in our approach to knowledge, to human values and hence to educational planning, we must be more hesitant and tentative than rationalist perspectives permit.

Indeed, the process approach to the curriculum represents an attempt to translate into curricular terms that notion of democracy which we noted earlier was advocated by John Dewey as the only appropriate social and educational context for the continued evolution of knowledge, values and society. It does not predetermine what pupils are to learn or the forms of behaviour they are to acquire. Rather it seeks to create the conditions under which they can grow and develop as individual, autonomous beings. It thus accepts that they have a role to play in their own education, that they must be active participants in it rather than passive recipients of it, that the curriculum must be negotiated with them, and that, above all, they must be encouraged to challenge what is presented to them as knowledge, to adopt a critical stance towards it, to question the grounds of its validity and to recognize its impermanence and its evolutionary nature.

Such a curriculum seeks to adopt a 'post-modern' view of change by creating the kind of open system which such a view entails, by allowing for a view of the development of human knowledge as transformatory rather than as accumulative or instrumental, and by acknowledging the complexity not only of the educational process but of human thought itself.

It is thus the only concept of curriculum and the only approach to curriculum planning which is consonant and compatible with this kind of view of knowledge and with this concept of change – change as inevitable, change as reflecting a continuing impermanence, change as neither good nor bad but simply as a recognizable part of the world and of human existence within it.

If that is our concept of change, we must be intellectually committed to a tentative – an empiricist or pragmatist – view of knowledge and values, to a recognition of the importance of democratic structures, for society and for schools, not only to provide individual freedom but also to promote the continued evolution of knowledge and values, and to a process model of curriculum as the only route to translating these commitments into curricular practice, in order to ensure and maintain those democratic structures and thus to promote the continued evolution of human knowledge and of human values.

If we have different views of knowledge, we will adopt different approaches to education. Conversely, if we have different views of education, this must imply that we have different views of knowledge (or that we have given insufficient thought to both). Thus a National Curriculum which prestates, predetermines and predefines its content and its 'aims and objectives' cannot be compatible with a view of knowledge as evolutionary or of change as continuous and inevitable, or, indeed, with any fundamentally viable concept of democracy. It reflects either a different, non-democratic ideology, or an intellectual impoverishment, a lack of adequate consideration of the issues involved. In the long term it cannot promote the continued development of education, of knowledge or of society. Whatever its intentions are, this can never be its effect. Indeed, its actual effect must be to inhibit such development.

## SUMMARY AND CONCLUSIONS

This chapter has attempted to show how important it is for every approach to educational change and innovation to begin from a careful analysis of the concept of change, and it has sought to explain why this is so.

It began by outlining several different concepts of change, and their resultant responses to the phenomenon of change, which can be discerned in the development of Western philosophical thought. In particular, it highlighted the contrast between those rationalist attempts to set up complex metaphysical systems in order to impose some form of permanence on changing phenomena and to offer explanations of them in terms of some wider, overarching scheme of things, and those empiricist forms of epistemology which reject all such metaphysical speculation, along with those 'post-modern' views which have challenged the knowledge paradigm of Newtonian physics and are thus forced to recognize change merely as a fact of existence with no underlying explanation, rationale or purpose.

The chapter then went on to claim that much of the technological advance of the twentieth century can be attributed to an acceptance of the second of these positions, and, in particular, to a recognition of the evolutionary nature of human knowledge and understanding.

We next noted that technological change cannot, or at least does not, occur in isolation from other aspects of human existence, and that, in particular, it is always associated with parallel changes in human values – aesthetic, moral, social and political. We suggested that any curriculum which is to take proper account of changing technology must recognize the necessity of taking on board these wider dimensions of change which technological change brings with it.

This led us to a consideration of the implications of these differing views of change for education, and it was proposed that, if we accept the view of change as fact, and thus of knowledge and values as in a continuous state of evolution, although not within any identifiable scheme or pattern, then education must seek to prepare pupils for the fact of change, by helping them to become adaptable – in all aspects of their lives – and it must also promote the continued evolution of knowledge and values by creating a democratic context to permit and encourage continuous challenge to whatever counts as knowledge at any particular time.

This took us finally to a consideration of different concepts of curriculum and approaches to curriculum planning in order to discover which of these might support and which might inhibit these developments. We noted here that both the content and the 'aims and objectives' models, whether operated separately or in tandem, are predicated on a view of knowledge which does not make proper allowance for its tentative and hypothetical status, since both begin by predetermining the knowledge-content to be transmitted and/or the behavioural changes to be brought about. Neither allows for change, modification or adaptation, and thus neither creates an educational context either for assisting pupils to become adaptable or for promoting in them a flexible stance towards human knowledge and values.

We concluded that a process view of curriculum and approach to curriculum planning, which does not prespecify anything more than the principles which are to underpin not only our initial planning but also our subsequent practice, which accepts the notion of curriculum negotiation, which seeks to offer a basis for continuous modification and which is itself positively predicated on the notion of the tentative nature of knowledge and values, is the only concept of curriculum which is compatible with a concept of change as an inevitable feature of human existence and one to be embraced rather than resisted.

The prime purpose of this discussion has been to establish the importance of assuring ourselves of a clear concept of change before we embark on the process of attempting to bring it about in any sphere, not least in order to ensure that what we do is compatible with our concept of change, or, at least, that it does not assume a view of change which, on analysis, we would not wish to subscribe to. It was thus intended to provide a conceptual base for a consideration of the empirical realities of change, especially in education; it is to these that we will turn in Chapter 3. First, however, we must familiarize ourselves with the theoretical perspectives which have emerged from studies of the practice of curriculum change, attempts to create a theoretical framework for analyzing and undertaking the process of educational change. This is the role of Chapter 2.

# 2

# EDUCATIONAL CHANGE: A THEORETICAL OVERVIEW

In Chapter 1 we argued that an understanding of the different philosophical interpretations which have been placed on the phenomenon of change, and the implications those different interpretations have for the conceptualization of change in education, is an essential prerequisite for effective practice. We suggested that our view of change in education must match our concept of change itself if our attempts to bring about educational change are to demonstrate consistency and coherence.

This chapter sets out to explore a second, related set of theoretical issues, an understanding of which, we would claim, is equally essential for effective practice. These theoretical issues have arisen not from attempts at conceptualizing change but from an analysis of the many strategies which have been adopted to implement it, especially in the field of education. For the theoretical understandings which have emerged from studies such as this not only represent analyses of practice but also provide several conceptual frameworks within which we can undertake such analyses. They are thus essential not only to the planning of change but also to the examination of the realities of curriculum change which we will undertake in Chapters 3 and 4.

The chapter divides into two broad general sections. First, we will explore theories of change which derived from early studies of attempts to change the school curriculum, studies which focused largely on strategies for bringing about such change and their relative effectiveness. Second, we will review more recent emerging perspectives which have been developed as these studies have been broadened to embrace not only strategies for change but also the need for a wider understanding of the nature of the change process, the complexities of human interactions which it involves and the kinds of barriers which exist to block the implementation of change. An understanding of the subtle aspects of educational change such as these perspectives offer is essential if we are to bring about real change in the curriculum rather than that superficial form of cosmetic change with which recent years have made us all too familiar.

Over the last thirty years a vast body of theoretical and research literature has been generated which reflects a world-wide concern with the process of change in educational institutions. This literature is not confined to Western industrialized countries. There is a burgeoning body of literature which addresses the process of educational change in so-called 'developing' countries. An interesting aspect of this literature is the universality of some of the themes that emerge, regardless of the context or geographical location in which it is generated. At the same time it highlights some important contextual differences. A considerable part of this literature is concerned with the elucidation of theoretical typologies or models which attempt to provide a conceptual framework for analysing the process of change. These typologies are invariably abstractions derived from an examination of empirically grounded instances *of* change. In turn, they have provided educational policy-makers and practitioners with possible strategies *for* promoting change. Thus the models have descriptive, prescriptive and explanatory usage. There is ample evidence available to demonstrate that a number of endeavours to bring about change in the curriculum of schools have utilized the insights these models offer.

## CURRICULUM CHANGE – THE BACKGROUND

Before examining the literature of change in detail, it would be helpful to explore briefly the concept of change in terms of how it has been used in relation to the curriculum. Change has been described as 'a generic term embracing a whole family of concepts' (Prescott and Hoyle, 1976, p. 27). Used in this context, change is a value neutral concept. The term in itself implies no qualitative judgement about the phenomenon to which it refers. However, the concepts that it embodies – such as innovation, development, renewal, reform, improvement – have more precise, qualitative meanings. Stenhouse for example, makes a clear distinction between innovation and renewal, arguing that curriculum renewal is a matter of updating materials, of keeping pace with developments of knowledge and techniques of teaching. Curriculum innovation involves changes in premises of teaching – its aims and values – and consequent thinking and classroom practice. This is an important distinction to highlight for much of what has been claimed in the name of curriculum innovation has often turned out, on closer inspection, to be curriculum renewal. A further distinction could be made between innovation and development. The former implies a radical break with former practice, the latter a more gradual enhancement of it. A number of these concepts also serve as reminders of the centrality of values in educational discourse. Improvement, for example, implies that new practices are not just different from what went before but that they are qualitatively better.

Fullan (1982) points out that curriculum change is not a single entity; it is multidimensional. He identifies three dimensions of change: namely, the use of new materials, the use of new teaching approaches, and the alteration of beliefs such as pedagogical assumptions and underlying theories. It is clear that the first two dimensions correspond to Stenhouse's conception of renewal and the third to his conception of innovation.

What this highlights is an important distinction between superficial and substantive change. Superficial change results in little more than new ways of categorizing or packaging familiar products. Substantive change affects the deeper structures of the curriculum and implies a fundamental reordering of categorical meanings. Cuban (1990) makes a similar distinction between first-order and second-order changes. First-order changes focus on the surface features of schooling in an effort 'to make what already exists more efficient and more effective' (op.cit., p. 73). Second-order changes address the structures of schooling and 'seek to alter the fundamental ways in which organizations are put together' (ibid.). In addition, it is possible to distinguish between different levels of curriculum change. Thus change may be located at the level of the classroom, the school, the local authority or the nation.

Although not without considerable overlap, it is possible to identify three distinct phases in curriculum change literature of British origin. The first phase coincided with the curriculum movement of the late 1960s and early 1970s. This movement was characterized primarily by endeavours to change the curriculum through the auspices of centrally funded agencies, in Britain almost exclusively the Schools Council. The second stage emerged during the late 1970s and continued into the 1980s as schools responded to encouragement and opportunities from various sources to become their own change agents. At present, an embryonic third stage is discernible as schools grapple with the realities of a centrally prescribed curriculum. Ironically, at the same time schools in some European countries are having to adjust to the luxury of a greater degree of autonomy in curriculum decision-making. Research suggests that such adjustment is a painful process following a tradition of centrally prescribed curriculum.

It would be misleading to imply that all schools participated in Schools Council projects or were the recipients of their products. Nor did all schools engage subsequently in school-initiated change. What has now to be confronted in England and Wales is the stark reality that all schools, whether they approve or not, have to face up to the realities of the changes brought about by the implementation of a centrally prescribed curriculum. In doing so, useful insights can be gleaned from the literature of the USA and continental Europe in that it reflects a long tradition of attempts to promote change within the constraints imposed by mandated curricula.

Early attempts to promote curriculum change systematically, and subsequently to research and explain the process, relied heavily on the work of a small group of American theorists. Of particular significance were Schon (1971), Havelock (1971), Bennis, Benne and Chin (1969) and House (1974). They themselves acknowledged the work of earlier theorists (e.g. Miles, 1964; Rogers, 1962) and developed many of their ideas from research findings in fields other than education. Their contribution to curriculum change theory has been cogently summarized elsewhere (MacDonald and Walker, 1976) but for the purpose and clarity of this book it needs to be restated and, where appropriate, re-examined with the hindsight of subsequent events. We make no apologies for this despite our concern that we may stand accused of peddling 'sixties speak' that has no relevance to the 'new realities' of the 1990s. If so, on three counts our defence is simple.

First, intellectual ideas, unlike perishable supermarket products, do not come conveniently stamped with a sell-by date although, as we shall see in Chapter 5, to suggest that they do is an important rhetorical device by which the purveyors of new policies attempt to sell us their wares. The appropriateness of an idea should be judged not by its age but by its efficacy to continue promoting understanding or clarifying human affairs. Past events, together with their associated ideas, are not discrete and static entities frozen in time. They form part of a dialectical relationship between past, present and possible futures. Present events and future possibilities are illuminated in the light of their historical antecedents. Conversely, our understanding of the past is transformed in the light of the unfolding present. The purpose of a historical perspective is not to record past events but to create a continuing conversation between past, present and future. In this process the meanings and usages of ideas are transformed. As Goodson and Walker (1991, p. xii) so succinctly put it, 'our intention in looking back is to search for new ways of looking forward'. Or in the words of Becker (1955, p. 189), 'the past is a kind of screen upon which we project our vision of the future'.

Second, in reviewing these frameworks we hope to provide a set of conceptual constructs and a shared language through which the process of educational change can be meaningfully analysed. They provide beacons in relation to which the literature on educational change can be fixed. No doubt the frameworks reviewed will eventually be superseded by ones of greater explanatory power. So far we would claim they have only been modified or supplemented. It should be pointed out that some interpretative licence is inevitable when ideas are synthesized independent of the contexts in which they were developed. For this reason readers may find it helpful at times to consult the original texts.

Third, it is plain to see that the understanding which has been generated about educational change has failed to penetrate the consciousness of many educationalists and most politicians for they persist in attempting to promote educational change through strategies which have proved to be ineffective in the past. At a time of unprecedented change in education, it does no harm to remind all concerned with educational policy-making of the legacy of understanding that is available.

## EARLY THEORIES OF CURRICULUM CHANGE

One of the most significant early contributions to the theory of curriculum change was that of Schon, although his work did not derive specifically from an educational context. In *Beyond the Stable State* (1971) Schon argues that modern industrial society is undergoing disruptive transition as a consequence of exponential technological change. Moreover, this technological change has become increasingly pervasive and now penetrates all aspects of life. New technology differs from that which preceded it on two counts. First, much new technology is 'infrastructure' technology which governs the flow of goods, people, money and information. Second, the most powerful new technologies are 'meta' technologies which, by facilitating the process of technological innovation and diffusion, increase the leverage society has on technological change itself. Thus society and all its institutions are in continuing processes of transformation. The consequence of this is the loss of stability – or what Schon terms 'the stable state' – at both the personal and institutional level. Some respond to this loss by seeking a return to the last stable state, others by revolting against established institutions. Schon contends that the constructive response is to confront the phenomenon directly by learning to understand, guide, influence and manage the transformations and by developing institutions which are 'learning systems' capable of bringing about their own continuing transformation. The task in short is 'to learn about learning' (op.cit., p. 30).

Schon then turns his attention to 'systems for diffusion' which he claims are 'critical to the learning capacity of a society' (op.cit., p. 80). It is this aspect of his work that has been most prominent in the development of educational change theory. Central to his thesis is the view that 'diffusion of innovation is a dominant model for the transformation of societies according to which innovation moves out from one or more points to permeate the society as a whole' (ibid.). He then proceeds to identify and examine a number of evolving models for the diffusion of innovation.

The centre–periphery model rests on three basic assumptions. First, the innovation exists, fully realized in its essentials, prior to its diffusion. Second, diffusion is the movement of an innovation from a centre out to its ultimate user, and, third, directed diffusion is a centrally managed process of dissemination, training, and provision of resources and incentives. The effectiveness of the model depends on the level of resources and energy at the centre, the number of points at the periphery, the length of the radii through which diffusion takes place, the energy required to gain a new adoption, and the capacity of the system for generating and monitoring feedback from the periphery. Failure occurs when the system exceeds the resources or energy at the centre, overloads the capacity of the radii or mishandles feedback from the periphery.

The proliferation-of-centres model is an elaboration of the centre–periphery model, designed to extend the limits and overcome the sources of failures inherent in the latter. It 'retains the basic centre–periphery structure but differentiates primary from secondary centres' (op.cit., p. 84). The secondary centre assumes responsibility for the diffusion of innovations. The primary centre specializes in training, deployment, support, monitoring and management. Its role is 'a trainer of trainers' (op.cit., p. 85). In effect, the proliferation-of-centres model multiplies the reach and efficiency of the diffusion system.

Writing in 1971, Schon claimed that the centre-periphery model and its extension the proliferation-of-centres model was 'not only historically important' but had also become 'the dominant normative model for diffusion' (op.cit., p. 94). However, he warned that a normative theory of diffusion based on this model had inadequacies beyond its actual historical failings. Even so, centre–periphery models or derivants have been – and continue to be – widely used in endeavours to effect educational change. Stenhouse (1975), among others, claims that the proliferation-of-centres model corresponded most closely to the facts of curriculum development initiatives carried out in England and Wales during the 1960s and early 1970s. The utilization of teachers' centres by the Schools Council for purposes of dissemination clearly supports this claim, although, as Stenhouse points out, they 'were associated administratively, not with the primary centres, but with enduring structures in the receiving system, the local authorities' (op.cit., p. 217). More recently, the National Council for Educational Technology involved university departments of education as secondary training centres in an attempt to disseminate its centrally produced Learning Geography Through Computers Project. Likewise, recent attempts to disseminate new initiatives, such as the General Certificate of Secondary Education (GCSE), through 'cascade' forms of training are clearly in keeping with the logic, if not the detail, of the proliferation-of-centres model. Centre–periphery assumptions are also built into the strategies used by the National Curriculum Council and the School Examinations and Assessment Council for supporting the implementation of the National Curriculum. The vast quantities of statutory and non-statutory guidance materials emanating from these bodies, and literally inundating schools, bears witness to this. And, as Schon astutely observes, 'the secret of mass production and distribution is also the secret of centre–periphery government' (op.cit., p. 252).

The third model of diffusion that Schon identifies he inelegantly terms 'the movement'. It is more commonly referred to as the shifting-centres model in the curriculum change literature. Unlike centre–periphery systems of diffusion, the movement has no clearly established centre, neither is there a stable, centrally established message. Centres rise and fall around new issues and leaders; doctrines shift and evolve. In the movement there is no stable structure through which an established message is diffused from the centre to the periphery. Rather, it is 'a loosely connected, shifting and evolving whole in which centres come and go and messages emerge, rise and fall' (op.cit., p. 112).

And because of the movement's capacity for self-transformation, it is 'survival-prone'. It continues to function with vitality even though all is in a state of flux around it. A number of movements in education correspond closely to this model, the most notable perhaps being that of action research. Other educational initiatives that share many of the characteristics of the model include integrated humanities and pastoral care.

Unlike that of Schon, the work of Havelock focuses more specifically on the process of educational change. His typology for explaining and promoting innovation is based on a review of 4,000 empirical studies of actual instances of innovation, although many of these relate to fields other than education. From this review he concludes that there are three main 'models', 'orientations' or 'perspectives' which are used to describe the dissemination and utilization of knowledge. These he terms 'research, development and diffusion' (RD&D), 'social interaction' (SI) and 'problem solving' (PS).

The RD&D model looks at the process from the perspective of the 'originator' or 'developer' of the innovation (MacDonald and Walker, 1976; Zaltman, Floria and Sikorski, 1977), who formulates a solution in response to an identified user need. The model embodies a number of assumptions. The process of innovation is regarded as a rational sequence of activities. The sequence begins with the researching of an identified problem, proceeds with the development and packaging of a solution and culminates with the mass dissemination of the solution to the targeted user. Planning is carried out on a massive scale, over a long time span. There is a clear division and co-ordination of labour. It assumes a rational consumer who will adopt the innovation if it fulfils a perceived need. Finally, high initial costs are accepted in anticipation of the long-term benefits in efficiency and quality of the innovation and its suitability for mass dissemination. Dissemination is perceived as a technical problem of finding the most effective means to facilitate the flow of the message from the centre to the periphery untainted. Havelock (1973) concludes that RD&D is most effective when adoption and translation problems in the user system are anticipated and adjusted for. In these circumstances the final outcome is 'user-proof' and 'guaranteed to work for the most feeble and incompetent receiver' (op.cit., p. 162).

The SI model emphasizes the pattern by which already existing innovations diffuse through a social system. Based on a large body of empirical research, the model supports five generalizations which Havelock claims have been demonstrated in a number of situations, including education. First, the individual adopter belongs to a network of social relationships which affects his/her adoptive behaviour. Second, the relative position of an individual adopter in this network is a good indicator of his/her rate of acceptance. Third, informal contact plays a crucial part in the adoption process. Fourth, group membership and group reference identifications are major predictors of individual adoptions. Fifth, the diffusion rate follows a predictable S-curve – slow initially, followed by a period of rapid diffusion, followed in turn by a long late adopter or 'laggard' period.

Both the RD&D and SI models assume that an innovation exists, fully developed, prior to its diffusion/dissemination to a largely passive user. In contrast, the PS model emphasizes the user as the initiator rather than the recipient of innovation. It regards innovation as a problem-solving process going on inside the user system. Problem solving is seen as a patterned sequence of activities which begins with the identification of a need. This need is translated into a problem statement and diagnosis. There then follows a search and retrieval of ideas and information, both inside and outside the user system, to assist in the fabrication of a solution. This solution is applied to practice and subsequently evaluated in terms of its effectiveness in satisfying the original need. The focus throughout the process is the need of the user; the role of the outsider is consultative or collaborative. Havelock claims that this is the model favoured by educational practitioners. He cites a number of derivatives (1973), including system self-renewal, action research, collaborative action enquiry and consultation. The nature and significance of these derivatives will become apparent in Chapter 4.

In our view, one of the most useful frameworks for analysing the process of change is that proposed by Bennis, Benne and Chin (1969). These writers delineate three groups of strategies for effecting change which they categorize as empirical–rational, normative–re-educative and power-coercive. Within each group a number of more specific strategies are identified and described. The significance of their work resides in the fact that they have provided a simple analytical framework capable of encapsulating, at a general level, virtually all the major approaches for promoting change which have been tried over the last thirty years.

Empirical–rational strategies are located within the general social orientation of the Enlightenment and classical liberalism which views ignorance and superstition as the main obstacles to rationality and progressive change. These strategies are predicated on the rather optimistic assumption that human beings are rational and that they will act according to their rational self-interest once this is revealed to them. The task of the change agent, therefore, is to demonstrate the validity of an innovation in terms of the increased benefits it offers the potential user. The exercise of rationality in the user system will then ensure its adoption. Foremost in this group is the RD&D strategy previously described but also of particular significance is the approach to change through the use of system analysis.

Normative–re-educative strategies perceive humans as inherently active and they emphasize the commitment that individuals invest in sociocultural norms and the patterns of action and practice that these norms support. According to this view, change is contingent upon practitioners discarding the normative orientations that inform their current practices and developing commitments to new ones.

Power-coercive strategies effect change through the application of power in some form or other, primarily political or economic but not necessarily so. Some coercive strategies emphasize the use of moral power. In essence, change is brought about through the 'compliance of those with less power to the plans, directions, and leadership of those with greater power' (op.cit., p. 23). Those who wish to bring about change mass political and economic power behind their change goals. And, as those who oppose the goals may utilize power in the same way to prevent change, power-coercive strategies are potentially divisive.

As indicated earlier, the three strategies identified by Bennis, Benne and Chin (1969) provide a useful framework for analysing curriculum change in Britain over the last thirty years. During the 1960s and early 1970s empirical–rational strategies predominated through the work of the Schools Council. In the mid-1970s this gave way to normative–re-educative strategies as the emphasis shifted to school-centred innovation. Throughout both these periods teachers enjoyed a considerable amount of autonomy in curriculum decision-making, particularly in the latter. In the earlier period, although teachers were not centrally involved in the development work of the Schools Council, their autonomy was respected in that they were under no obligation to adopt the resulting products. The 1980s were characterized by an unprecedented shift to power-coercive strategies, and a subsequent erosion of teacher autonomy, as central government intervened increasingly in curriculum matters; this shift culminated with a vengeance in the 1988 Education Reform Act and the subsequent implementation of the National Curriculum.

The typologies and models we have examined so far were formulated in response to the curriculum development initiatives of the 1960s and early 1970s. In recent years a number of writers have proposed alternative interpretative frameworks against which efforts to promote, research or theorize change can be made. These frameworks reflect a more sophisticated understanding of the complexity of the process and a more explicit but not exclusive concern with processes within schools which may facilitate change or militate against it. We will now examine this more recent work.

## RECENT AND EMERGENT THEORETICAL PERSPECTIVES

House (1979, 1981) claims that innovation studies have been generated from only a few overall perspectives. He identifies three perspectives– the technical, the cultural and the political–as the most dominant. Olson and Eaton (1987) identify three conceptions of change: the systems approach, the ecological and the reflexive. Adams, Cornbleth and Plank (1988) delineate 'three distinct but operationally overlapping sets of planning models'–the technicist, the political and the consensual – in relation to state reform efforts in the USA. These typologies offer important insights into the process of educational change and have been widely adopted for the purpose of analysis, particularly that of House. However, they fail to represent fully the complexity and diversity of the theoretical and research literature that has been generated on educational change. It is doubtful whether any one typology can successfully encapsulate all the phenomena with which it is concerned but we suggest that attempts to promote, research and analyse educational change are most adequately represented within the following six perspectives: the technological; the cultural; the micropolitical; the biographical; the structural; the sociohistorical.

Each perspective has its own implicit assumptions concerning the nature of change, of schools as institutions and of human agency. It would be wrong to assume that any one perspective offers a privileged or more accurate interpretation of how change occurs, how change could be more effectively promoted or how change is explained in educational institutions; descriptively, prescriptively and analytically they all have their merits and limitations. Neither should the perspectives be treated as discrete entities. Although each offers a unique set of insights into the change process, they clearly overlap and interrelate. They function, primarily, not as descriptors of empirical reality but as important heuristic devices in seeking to understand the nature and process of educational change.

## The technological perspective

The technological perspective emerged as the dominant means of conceptualizing and initiating change during the 1960s as the 'unplanned drift' of earlier years gave way to a more rational and systematic approach, as typified by the RD&D, centre–periphery or empirical–rational strategies described earlier in this chapter. These strategies assume schools to be rational organizations that are 'readily manipulated and easily changed' (Lieberman and Rosenholtz, 1987, p. 81). Teachers themselves are, at best, perceived as 'rational adopters' who will readily recognize the value of, and therefore implement, the proposals they are offered or, at worst, are treated as 'stoneage obstructionists' who have to be 'neutralized' through the use of teacher-proof materials (Ponder and Doyle, 1977).

Adherents to this perspective view the process of curriculum change as a form of instrumental action concerned with finding the most effective and efficient means of bringing about prestated intentions. Central to the perspective is the logic of technical rationality, an epistemology of practice derived from positivist philosophy which maintains that problems of practice are technical in character and that practitioners, therefore, are first and foremost instrumental problem solvers. Thus, in an educational context, professional practice is directed towards the resolution of well-formed instrumental problems through the systematic application of the theories and techniques of the empirical sciences (Schon, 1983, 1987). Closely associated with technical rationality – if not synonymous – is its bureaucratic counterpart, defined by MacIntyre (1985) as 'the rationality of matching means to ends economically and efficiently' (op.cit., p. 25).

Attempts have been made to explain the persistence and pervasiveness of technical rationality as a mode of thinking and acting. A number of writers see it as an integral part of the modern world – or 'modernity' – through which our existential realities are defined. The salient features of modernity are succinctly summarized by the editors of *Precis* (no. 6, 1987, pp. 7–24, quoted in Harvey, 1989) as follows: 'Generally perceived as positivistic, technocentric, and rationalistic universal modernism has been identified with the belief in linear progress, absolute truths, the rational planning of ideal social orders, and the standardization of knowledge and production'.

So, technical rationality does not just inform the modern world; it is the very essence of modernity itself. And, as Aronowitz and Giroux (1986, p. 47), in synthesizing the work of Horkheimer (1947), comment, 'The restricted language and thought codes produced by the reduction of all thought to its technical dimension reach far into the culture, encompassing schools as well as communications, the public as well as the private spheres of discourse'. Thus, technical rationality generates and perpetuates its own distinctive discourse, the central metaphors of which are industrial and instrumental. As Oliver and Gershman (1989, p. 19) observe, 'metaphor provides the sustaining imagery (and consequent language) for what later becomes a conscious sense of culture. Our guess is that the root metaphor for modernity which drives our implicit commitment to the ideology of specialization, efficiency and technical knowledge is the *machine*'.

In Western industrial societies so entrenched is technical rationality and so pervasive the discourse it generates that it becomes difficult to conceive, let alone actualize, alternative forms of social and institutional life. The consequence of this for educational practice is neatly summarized by Giroux. He states:

> The growing removal of curriculum development and analysis from the hands of teachers is related to the ways technocratic rationality is used to redefine teachers' work. This type of rationality increasingly takes place within a social division of labour in which thinking is removed from implementation and the model of the teacher becomes that of the technician or white-collar clerk. Likewise, learning is reduced to the memorization of narrowly defined facts and isolated pieces of information that can easily be measured and evaluated.
>
> (Giroux, 1989, p. 180)

As well as its underpinning logic of technical rationality, the technological perspective has a number of other major deficiencies. First, it is assumed that innovators and classroom practitioners construe practice in the same way. Consequently, there is a failure to recognize and make allowance for the inevitable 'slippage' between the original conception of an innovation or policy initiative and the interpretation of it at the site of implementation. Second, the ideas of innovators or policy-makers are considered to be inherently superior to those of classroom practitioners. Teachers are perceived merely as 'cogs in the wheel' and their role is reduced to that of 'production line technocrats'. Third, important features of schools as organizations tend to be missed, obscured or downplayed. The established systems of meaning that exist in schools are invariably disregarded and any adverse reaction to innovation is typified, with negative connotations, as resistance to change. And, as Marris (1974, p. 155) points out, 'When those who have power to manipulate changes act as if they have only to explain, and when their explanations are not at once accepted, shrug off opposition as ignorance and prejudice, they express a profound contempt for the meaning of lives other than their own'. Fourth, the technological perspective embodies a limited and, in our opinion, distorting view of the curriculum. The curriculum is seen as a tangible product that can be planned and constructed independent of its transactional context. It is therefore assumed that to effect change involves little more than a change of product. Indeed, this assumption was explicit in the early work of the Schools Council. The central function of a project was seen as the production of new teaching materials in the belief that changing the content provided 'a vehicle for trying to deepen teachers' understanding of the teaching process' (Banks, 1969, p. 255). And, we would argue, similar simplistic assumptions are inherent in the thoughts and actions of those who support the imposition on schools of centrally prescribed curricula.

It might be implied from what we have said so far that from a technological perspective attempts to change schools are invariably through the initiatives of agencies external to the school. This is not necessarily the case. It is the logic which informs the procedures through which change is effected, rather than the locus of initiative, that characterizes the technological perspective. Thus, related to this perspective are those *internally* initiated approaches to change which emphasize the school as a functional organization which can be improved through the systematic application of prespecified procedures. Holt (1987) cites strategies such as organization development (OD) and Guidelines for Review and Institutional Development (GRIDS) as examples. These approaches to change will be examined in detail in Chapter 4.

In the early work of the Schools Council a techno–rational model of action dominated all stages of the innovation process, although there were notable exceptions. The overall change strategy adhered closely to the logic of RD&D. The planning of the innovation itself utilized an objectives model of planning, partly because no viable alternative had been articulated at the time but more crucially because the specification of objectives was perceived as being an essential prerequisite for rendering projects amenable to research evaluation (Banks, 1969).

Dissemination was seen as a technical problem of creating organizational structures and communication networks that would facilitate the flow of the message, hopefully untainted, from the developers at centre to the users at the periphery. This did not lead to the extreme, as in the USA, of teacher-proofing projects in order to safeguard their integrity. However, elaborate programmes were set up designed to bridge the gap in the understanding of an innovation between the developers and the users. This was attempted through a variety of means including the establishment of local networks, the appointment of regional co-ordinators, the running of local and national training and the use of schools involved in the trial phase as 'demonstration units' (Banks, op.cit.).

Despite prolonged dissemination efforts, RD&D strategies have achieved limited success – at least in terms of take-up – in educational systems. A number of theories have been forwarded to account for this lack of success. Initially the problem was perceived as one of dissemination. Later, attention turned to an examination of processes within the user system which were believed to influence the adoption and successful implementation of an innovation. Failure, initially, was explained as a generalized resistance within the user system: the 'dynamic conservatism', which we noted in Chapter 1, by which institutions 'fight to remain the same' (Schon, 1971, p. 32). Alternatively, such resistance was characterized as a pathological response of individuals. Research has exposed the resistance explanation as somewhat simplistic. There is well-documented evidence suggesting that many schools, and individual teachers, welcome change if it appears to offer a solution to an identified need; indeed, in such circumstances they are often the instigators of change. Gross, Giacquinta and Bernstein (1971), for example, demonstrate that an initiative to promote change in a school, although ultimately unsuccessful, had been initially welcomed by the teaching staff. However, for a number of reasons, both organizational and interpersonal, resistance emerged as a problem as the innovation developed. Consequently, they rejected the resistance hypothesis as the main determinant of failure and sought to identify other contextual factors inhibiting change.

Rosario provides a succinct summary of the alternative explanations that have been advanced to account for the phenomenon of resistance.

> In explaining this phenomenon, some look to individual psychology, pointing to such personality-maintaining factors as habit, selective perception, insecurity, and so on. Others argue that the

reasons for resistance are more related to the nature of schools as formal organizations. For these, schools are complex social systems whose properties make them virtually impenetrable to change. Such properties include domestication, role invisibility, situational imperatives and loose coupling, among others. Still others maintain that the problem of school resistance is traceable to cultural features of the school. Schools in this case are seen as cultural entities in themselves, with norms, rules and behavioral regularities that function to inhibit change.

(Rosario, 1986, p. 39)

Resistance then can be explained, not as some generalized institutional characteristic or individual disposition, but as a consequence of a complex interplay of biographical, organizational or cultural factors. These perspectives will be examined in turn in the course of this chapter.

## The cultural perspective

This perspective, in contrast to the technological, treats educational organizations as cultural entities, as 'complex social organizations held together by a symbolic webbing rather than a formal system driven by goals, official roles, commands and rules' (Deal, 1990, p. 7). Whilst the technological perspective emphasizes the management of change, the cultural perspective is more concerned with its meaning (Rudduck, 1986a). It locates and examines the process of change within the sociocultural milieu of educational practice and one of its central concerns is 'the meaning of teaching to teachers and the origins of those meanings' (Feiman-Nemser and Floden, 1986, p. 505). Its basic premise implies that 'innovation cannot be assimilated unless its meaning is shared' (Marris, 1974, p. 113).

The term culture is notoriously difficult to define, especially when applied to education. As Gibson (1986, p. 66) claims, 'culture is one of the most complex and elusive concepts we possess'. Consequently, the term 'is often applied to schools with a wilful lack of precision' (Nias, 1989, p. 143). Trumbull (1989, p. 458) defines school culture as 'the *standard practices*, the *meanings* assigned to these practices, and the *processes* that establish and maintain these practices and meanings'. For Corbett, Firestone and Rossman (1987, p. 40) it is 'the shared expectations of what is and what ought to be'. In common parlance it is simply 'the way we do things around here' (Deal and Kennedy,

1983, p. 4). It is beyond the scope of this book to analyse in depth the different interpretations of culture. However, it is clear from these definitions that school culture is perceived as having both an interpretative and normative function. It provides the contextual clues through which events and actions are interpreted by institutional members and, simultaneously, it regulates the way they are expected to behave. Culture gives meaning and purpose to human endeavour by providing a degree of stability, certainty and predictability (Deal, 1987). And, as we will discuss later in this chapter, the norms, beliefs and values that constitute this culture provide the framework both within and through which teachers construct, legitimate and preserve their professional identities.

Words and terms used in defining culture – 'standard practices', 'shared expectations', 'core values', 'regularities', etc. – seem to imply that cultures are homogeneous entities, persistent over time and space. This is clearly not true of cultures in general nor of school cultures in particular. Admittedly, the nature of schooling is such that teachers do, to a significant extent, share a common occupational culture. But, as Feiman-Nemser and Floden (1986, p. 50) argue, 'the assumption of cultural uniformity is . . . untenable', for teachers, in terms of age, experience, sociocultural background, ethnicity, gender and personal circumstances, display diverse characteristics. Nor are the schools they occupy homogeneous. Among other things, they vary in size, situation, architecture, pupils' age range, and internal organization. Consequently, as research demonstrates (Rossman, Corbett and Firestone, 1988), there are considerable variations both between and within schools in the uniformity of their cultures. Rather than homogeneous entities, schools are sites where a number of different cultures intersect and interact. According to Rossman, Corbett and Firestone (1988, p. 122) 'the issue is one of figure and ground. From a distance a sameness overwhelms; from closer up, variation is striking'. Moreover, cultures are, to varying degrees, dynamic. Schools have witnessed considerable change in their technologies and social relationships and, while substantive changes in the deeper meanings of schooling may be less apparent, the cultural perspective at least acknowledges the possibility of such transformations.

Nor are the norms, beliefs and values that constitute school cultures all of equal significance. Corbett, Firestone and Rossman (1987) draw an important distinction between norms that are 'sacred' and those that are 'profane' (see also Rossman, Corbett and Firestone, 1988). The former are 'essentially immutable' (Rossman, Corbett and

Firestone, 1988, p. 10): the teachers' bottom line. Changes that challenge these norms 'represent attacks on professional raison d'etre, on the cornerstones of teachers' constructions of reality' (op.cit., p. 12). Consequently such changes may be met initially with 'forthright resistance' (Corbett, Firestone and Rossman, 1987, p. 36) and, if the challenge persists, with 'the creation of a culture of opposition' (ibid.). By comparison, profane norms are less deeply embedded and, 'although occupying strategic positions in the day-to-day world' (Rossman, Corbett and Firestone, 1988, p. 11), are susceptible to change, some more so than others.

This distinction provides a useful basis for reconceptualizing a number of aspects of educational change, particularly the phenomenon of resistance. Resistance to change can now be explained as a lack of congruence between the existing school culture and the culture embedded in the change proposals. As Rudduck (1986b, p. 7) observes, 'in our efforts to change I think we have generally underestimated the power of the existing culture of the school and classroom to accommodate, absorb or expel innovations that are at odds with the dominant structures and values that hold habit in place'. The distinction also helps to explain the discrepancies in the 'take-up' of innovations which was evident in the work of the Schools Council. It implies that the more congruent an innovation is with a school's prevailing culture – or, conversely, the less it challenges the sacred norms – the greater are its chances of being successfully implemented. Thus, it seems reasonable to speculate that as subject-based innovations are more congruent with the epistemological beliefs and pedagogical practices of teachers, at least those in secondary schools, they create less 'cultural dissonance' and are therefore more likely to be accepted. But, ironically for the same reason, they are more easily assimilated into prevailing practice and lead only to superficial change or 'innovation without change' (MacDonald and Rudduck, 1971, p. 151). The most successful Schools Council project in terms of take-up, Geography for the Young School-Leaver (GYSL), is a case in point. Although departing in significant ways from traditional practice in terms of pedagogy, its content was, in essence, congruent with the culturally embedded epistemological assumptions of geography teachers. Dalton's study (1988) lends some credence to this claim. In one of the schools he studied, GYSL, although perceived as innovatory, had been assimilated into a set of fairly traditional classroom practices. In another school, practised within a progressive humanities department, the project was promoted and defended by 'reformed geographers' but derided as reactionary – and hence inimical to change – by a group of 'radicals' who rejected the logic of subject-based humanities courses. Members of this latter group contended that its supposedly innovatory 'key concepts' approach was essentially a form of 'new content'.

A number of researchers focus more specifically on the occupational culture of teaching and attempt to assess the implications of their findings for curriculum change. Of particular significance is the work of Lortie (1975). He describes the occupational culture of teaching as individualistic, present-oriented and conservative. In summarizing Lortie's work, Hargreaves (1989, p. 54) claims that 'teachers avoid long term planning and collaboration with their colleagues and resist involvement in whole school policy-making in favour of gaining marginal improvements in time and resources to make their own individual classroom work easier'. Other research confirms Lortie's findings, indicating that teachers in most schools remain isolated from one another and rarely discuss their classroom practices or seek collegial solutions to classroom problems (Heckman, 1987). This cult of privatism is reinforced by a work ethic that expects teachers to demonstrate a high degree of competency working in classrooms on their own. This expectation is hardly conducive to risk-taking, especially for those practitioners in the process of establishing their credibility in the profession. This syndrome reinforces itself. It has been shown that teachers are often reluctant to request assistance, or even to discuss their work, in the fear that this may be interpreted as a disclosure of professional inadequacy (Rosenholtz, 1985). Thus, cultures 'conspire to maintain the *status quo*' (Heckman, 1987, p. 77) and for many teachers the classroom becomes a sanctuary, 'preserved and protected through . . . isolation and a hesitancy of parents, administrators and other teachers to violate it' (Bullough, 1987, p. 93).

Privatism is reinforced by the egg-crate architectural structures of schools, with isolated and insulated classroom compartments, and by cellular patterns of organization (Lortie, 1975). Weick (1976) characterizes schools as 'loosely coupled systems' in which each element is attached but retains some identity and separateness. While these structures ensure a degree of autonomy for organizational members, they reduce the potential for collaborative action. The constraints of inadequate resources, poor buildings and large classes, together with the confrontational nature of pupil–teacher interactions (Lortie, 1975), means that teachers are 'caught in a defensive battle for day-to-day survival' (Hargreaves, D.H. 1982, p. 208). Within these constraints they acquire a limited repertoire of narrow but stable and apparently 'successful' working practices which become extremely resistant to change. It is little wonder, therefore, that teachers often lack the skills and the inclination to participate in whole school decision-making. As Sarason (1982, p. 162) puts it, 'The teacher is alone with problems and dilemmas, constantly thrown back on personal resources, having little or no interpersonal vehicles available for purposes of stimulation, change or control'.

The centrality of the classroom in the occupational culture of teaching is an interesting and well-documented phenomenon. Research suggests that teachers rely almost exclusively on practical classroom experience as the main source of their professional knowledge and give little credence to formal educational theory (Hargreaves, 1984). It is claimed that teachers' psychic rewards come largely from classroom interactions with pupils (Lortie, 1975) despite, it seems, the apparent antagonistic nature of these interactions. Even when opportunities arise for teachers to engage collaboratively with colleagues, many show a marked reluctance to do so. In a group of elementary schools in Canada, Hargreaves (1990a, 1990b) found that many teachers reacted negatively to the provision of additional preparation time in that they perceived it as potentially disruptive to the continuity or 'flow' of their classroom practice. Moreover, the additional time tended to be used by teachers to deal with the exigencies of their classrooms rather than for the purpose of long-term collaborative planning.

Rudduck (1984, 1986a) contends that the inertia of past meaning is a formidable barrier to change and, consequently, effective change is dependent on building new meaning within the working group. She extends the notion of the working group to include pupils and examines innovation from their perspective. Many children have a very instrumental view of education and develop strong expectations of what constitutes appropriate pedagogical practices and curriculum content (Edwards, 1983). Therefore, they do not necessarily understand or share the meanings inherent in innovative educational practices. Unfortunately, teachers are inclined to assume that their authority is sufficient to justify change and they fail to enter into discussion with their pupils about the meanings inherent in the changes they are attempting to bring about. Deviation from expected norms is disorienting to pupils and to preserve their structures of meaning they will attempt to force the teacher to reinstate practices with which they are more familiar (Rudduck, 1986a).

Once the cultural realities of schools are recognized it is possible to conceptualize the process of change in a more sophisticated way. The cultural norms that inform the practice of teachers are deeply rooted but, to a large extent, implicit and intuitive. As Erickson (1987, p. 18) argues, 'it is precisely that which makes intuitive sense to someone that is evidence of some aspect of the individual's cultural system'. Teachers are too familiar with the cultural norms of their occupation to appreciate the hold they exercise over them. They are blinded by familiarity in the way that the fish, presumably, is the last creature to understand the nature of water. Professional understanding can be enhanced, however, through procedures which help teachers confront the norms embedded in their practice. This requires procedures which distance teachers from their taken-for-granted realities. The familiar has to be made strange. The key to promoting change is through the establishment of collaborative cultures, based on the principles of collegiality, openness and trust (Lieberman and Miller, 1990), for 'schools cannot be improved without people working together' (Lieberman, 1986, p. 6). In such cultures a norm prevails 'that favors the thoughtful, explicit examination of practices and their consequences' (Little, 1990, p. 522). In Porter's view (1987, p. 150), collaborative practices 'break down teacher isolation and give credence to their ideas; make them more receptive to and analytical with new ideas; increase professional confidence; [and] strengthen commitment to the improvement of practice'.

Little (1990) distinguishes between different kinds of teachers' collegial relations on an independent–interdependent continuum. At the independent end collegial relations are confined to 'story telling and scanning for ideas'. While story telling may have some cathartic value, it remains doubtful whether it contributes much to teachers' professional understanding. Moving towards the interdependence end of the continuum, collegial relations become more interactive through 'aid and assistance' and 'sharing'. The greatest degree of interdependence, however, is achieved through 'joint work'. Little (op.cit., p. 519) reserves this term for 'encounters among teachers that rest on shared responsibility for the work of teaching (interdependence), collective conceptions of autonomy, support for teachers' initiative and leadership with regard to professional practice, and group affiliations grounded in professional work'. This again implies that substantive change in the curriculum is contingent upon a fundamental reorientation in school culture. As Deal (1990, p. 9) observes, 'schools will become fundamentally different only when we quit correcting surface deficiencies and recognize that transformation involves a collective renegotiation of historically anchored myths, metaphors and meanings'.

It is doubtful, though, whether collaboration in itself is enough to guarantee significant change in classroom practice. As currently prac-tised, collaboration is largely voluntary and often focuses on those areas of school life that are generally peripheral and uncontested. Alternatively, collaboration may operate at the level of policy-making with policy implementation being carried out on an individual basis. Collaboration, then, is not an end in itself but an important pre-requisite to the development of 'a culture of inquiry' (Lieberman and Miller, 1990). It is the disposition to enquiry rather than collaboration *per se* that provides the catalyst for change. This is an important distinction to make for it is being advocated that the implementation of the National Curriculum in Britain will require teachers to adopt more collaborative working practices. At one level this is likely to be true. What is at issue here is not collaboration itself but the ends to which it will be directed. It is predictable, perhaps inevitable, that collaboration will be directed primarily towards solving the largely technical prob-lem of translating the requirements of the National Curriculum into workable classroom practices. In these circumstances collaboration does not serve the emancipatory interests of teachers but becomes a hegemonous tool for the use of those in power to ensure that their policies are effectively implemented. This kind of collaboration Hargreaves (1990a) terms 'contrived collegiality' which, he contends, 'may be much more compatible with the purposes of administrative control than with those more vaunted ones of teacher empowerment' (op.cit., p. 5). As such, conservatism and privatism could be seen in a more positive light, providing an antidote to the 'quick-fix' approaches to educational policy-making favoured by politicians and bureaucrats. Contrary to the almost universal assumption of Western thought, as we saw in Chapter 1, not all change is virtue. Consequently, it is impera-tive that proposals for educational change, whatever and wherever their origins, are scrutinized in relation to fundamental questions of value and purpose.

These issues are becoming increasingly a focus of research in Britain following the implementation of the National Curriculum in England and Wales. This legislation represents a radical departure from a long-standing tradition of individual and institutional autonomy and will inevitably have some impact on the cultures of schools. But, sig-nificantly, the reverse is also true. Centralist policies will, to varying degrees, undergo transmutations as they are mediated through prevail-ing school cultures. In this respect the work of Broadfoot *et al.* (1988) and Acker (1990) is of particular interest. In a case study of a primary school, Acker (op.cit.) analyses the way the culture shaped its response to the National Curriculum. She found that certain aspects of the culture impeded implementation; other features, such as its collegial, collaborative style, reduced short-term anxieties and made implementation smoother. But again, as Acker hints, in assessing the significance of these findings, we have to be vigilant as to whose interests, in the long term, are being served.

Broadfoot *et al.* (op.cit.) contrast the occupational cultures of a number of comparative primary schools in England and France. The former have developed in a climate of relative autonomy in curriculum decision-making; the latter in response to a nationally prescribed, but generally accepted, curriculum. The research demonstrates that the contrasting contexts induced in teachers crucial differences in how they conceived their professional responsibilities. Compared with their counterparts in England, teachers in France demonstrated a more limited and more classroom-focused conception of their role, as a consequence of their duties being contractually defined. In England teaching was seen as 'problematic'; in France 'axiomatic' or self-evident. The data suggested a strong emphasis on the process of learning in England. In France a product view of learning prevailed. Finally differences were found in the goals set for pupils in the respective countries. Teachers in France emphasized basic cognitive skills while in England the goals of teachers were more universalistic.

Broadfoot *et al.* (op.cit.) argue that the imposition of a national curriculum in England and Wales could result in all the disadvantages found in the French system and, additionally, create 'widespread resentment and disquiet' (op.cit., p. 283) in that it requires teachers to 'adopt a professional role that is alien to them' (ibid.). We would not wish to disagree.

## The micropolitical perspective

A number of writers argue that the perspectives so far examined provide inadequate accounts of schools and, by implication, of the processes that take place within them, including change. These perspectives tend to treat schools as homogeneous entities, thus masking important internal conflicts and tensions. The cultural perspective does acknowledge the possibility of subcultures but these are often perceived as being subordinate to an all-pervasive dominant culture. It continues to privilege consensus over conflict as an explanatory device. Ironically, the move towards more collaborative cultures often has the

effect of making the micropolitics of schools more visible. Conflicting interests are often an expression of the competing subculture
ideologies 'with proponents of competing views each holding their own
to serve the best interest of students' (Little, 1990, p. 521). In collaborative cultures deeply held beliefs – the sacred norms – are more
likely to be exposed. It is perhaps in order to minimize conflict that
collaboration tends to focus on those areas of school life that are
largely peripheral and uncontested. From a cultural perspective collaboration is perceived as a desirable end in itself; from a micropolitical perspective questions are raised concerning the ends and
interests it serves.

Hoyle (1982, p. 88) contends that 'politics is inevitably concerned
with interests'. For him, micropolitics 'embraces those strategies by
which individuals and groups in organizational contexts use their
resources of power and influence to further their interests' (ibid.).
Thus, from a micropolitical perspective, the distribution and utilization of power in educational institutions becomes the crucial issue in
attempting to understand the process of change. Schools and departments within them are viewed as 'arenas of struggle'. As various
factions pursue their conflicting interests, bargains are struck, alliances
formed and compromises made. Ideological differences and conflicting
interests are brought to the surface when attempts to promote change
are instigated.

The micropolitics of schools are manifested, primarily, in and
through those aspects of institutional life concerned with the control
of territory, the distribution of resources, the acquisition of status
and participation in the decision-making process. These provide the
material, symbolic and discursive resources and power through which
interests can be pursued.

From a micropolitical perspective change is seen as potentially –
perhaps inherently – destabilizing in that it invariably leads to a
rearrangement of the power relationships between individuals and
groups. And, as micropolitical research highlights, often 'desired
changes fall short because they threaten the balance of power, create
opposing coalitions and trigger conflict' (Deal, 1987, p. 7). Ball (1987,
p. 40) draws attention to the fact that 'change in policy should not be
confused with change in practice. In the micro-politics of the school it
is often the former which is at stake, although micro-political strategies
may also be deployed to promote or defend the other'. Moreover,
research shows that in a school the same change may have contradictory effects by increasing the power, both real and perceived, of some

groups and rendering others virtually powerless. As Sparkes (1989, p. 105) observes, in the process of innovation 'some teachers will define themselves as winners, some as losers and some as sideliners'.

From a micropolitical perspective, subject departments are seen as a most significant organizational and political division within the secondary school (Ball, 1989). Usually, but not always, they confer on their members a sense of common identity in relation to space, episteme and pedagogy; some more than others. The relative status and power of departments is, at the same time, a consequence of, and reflected in, the curricular structure of the school. For example, Richardson (1973, p. 196) notes the inequality between 'the modern languages and sciences departments on the one side and the geography and history departments on the other'. Micropolitical conflict is not only expressed through, but may be accentuated by, curricular structures of schools. For example, the structure of the 'options system' in many secondary schools encourages subject departments to compete, albeit covertly, for 'customers' and indirectly for material and human resources, time and territory. It will be interesting to observe the impact, if any, that the move to a more overtly subject-based curriculum, as a consequence of the implementation of the National Curriculum, has on the micropolitics of primary schools.

Although the curricular structures of schools have demonstrated marked resilience over time, they are in a constant state of tension, and subject to modification as micropolitical struggles and conflicts are played out. Undoubtedly, in many schools, humanities departments have been created and welcomed for strategic rather than philosophical reasons. At the same time, in other schools, small but independent subject departments have fiercely resisted subsumption into larger conglomerates as this is perceived to pose the greater threat to their long-term interests. The introduction of the National Curriculum creates the possibility of many new curricular configurations and alliances. Note the way Home Economics somewhat pragmatically secured its immediate future, and at the same time enhanced its status, by entering into a coalition, albeit as a junior partner, with Design and Technology.

It would be misleading to imply that subject departments are homogeneous units based on collegiate principles and shared values. They have their own divisions and conflicts and, as Dalton's (1988) study shows, when engaged in innovation they are not immune from internecine strife. Furthermore, his research demonstrates how, in a humanities department, differences of ideology and personality rather than subject allegiances tended to be the main source of conflict. Neither should it be assumed that in secondary schools the subject department is the main unit to which teachers belong. At a generalized level this may be the case, but from a micropolitical perspective it is important to recognize that teachers' allegiances are often to diverse constituencies. Allegiances to particular educational ideologies may transcend subject department boundaries. In most secondary schools teachers have commitments across the academic–pastoral divide. Some have teaching responsibilities in more than one subject department. Socially, teachers' strongest allegiance may be to colleagues from other departments, forged perhaps through commonality in age and experience, mutual interests or collective involvement in extra-curricular activities. In schools, faced with the demands of diverse allegiances, the maintenance of an institutional 'even keel' requires of its members the exercise of considerable political acumen.

Holt (1990) provides an interesting account of change from a micro-political perspective, although he does not designate it specifically as such. His case study highlights the conflicting interests, and resultant political manoeuvrings, within and between various committees set up in a school specifically to promote change. However, as Holt (op.cit., p. 143) observes, over a period of two years 'none of the changes that were expected . . . had actually occurred'. Endeavours to innovate were characterized by all talk and no action. The only change that did materialize was confined to the lower school and to non-academic aspects of the curriculum. His study implies that even in schools committed to a general policy of innovation vested interests often prevail over the common good.

Other case studies of the micropolitics of schools serve to demonstrate how power is exercised through the control and selective use of particular forms of discourse. Hargreaves, for example (1981), illustrates how a headteacher was able to manipulate the decision-making process through the use of a discursive practice he terms contrastive rhetoric. For Hargreaves (op.cit., p. 309), 'contrastive rhetoric refers to that interactional strategy whereby the bounds of normal and acceptable practice are defined by institutionally and/or interactionally dominant individuals or groups through the introduction into discussion of alternative practices and social forms in stylized, trivialized and generally pejorative terms which connote their unacceptability'. Thus, the legitimation and control of discourse is a central feature of the way power is exercised and interests are pursued in schools. The implication for change of other discursive practices will be examined in Chapter 5.

The micropolitical perspective provides no clear blueprint for bringing about change in schools, although it does provide useful insight into some of the inherent difficulties. Its contribution to our understanding of the process of change has been largely empirical and somewhat pessimistic. It offers no prescription other than the possibility of devising strategies for uniting factions around common goals. But once the micropolitical realities of schools are recognized, the pursuit of consensus and collegiality as democratic ideals has to be recognized as practically problematic. In sites characterized by value pluralism and unequal access to power, compromise rather than consensus prevails, and as compromise generally favours the powerful and privileged the status quo is maintained (Edwards, 1992). However, on a more optimistic note, it is well worth remembering that, in the words of MacIntyre (1985, p. 164), 'it is through conflict and sometimes only through conflict that we learn what our ends and purposes are'.

## The biographical perspective

The biographical perspective emphasizes the way in which change impinges upon the lives and careers of practitioners and how the two phenomena interact. It is centrally concerned with examining change in relation to the biographical experiences of individual practitioners, in terms of their hopes, aspirations, fears, commitments, beliefs and values. Appropriate research involves no less than getting inside the heads of practitioners to gain access to their thought processes in order to interpret the world from their perspective. Its analytical frameworks include personal construct and social interactionist theory; its methodologies utilize interview, questionnaire and observation and, more recently, autobiography, narrative and story.

It is now widely recognized that the success of curriculum innovation, whether internally or externally initiated, is contingent upon the professional development of teachers. Yet we have limited understanding of the teacher characteristics associated with the successful implementation of innovation (Stein and Wang, 1988; Rudduck, 1988). The tendency has been to examine the process of innovation at the institutional rather than the individual level. As Rudduck (op.cit., p. 208) points out, 'dealing with the individual's reaction to the possibility to change is not something that has attracted much attention in the literature of educational innovation'. Huberman (1988, p. 199) makes a similar observation: 'each innovation has been construed as a time-bound process, with little concern being shown for the prior and subsequent careers of the actors involved'.

The occupational context of teachers' lives is characterized by multi-dimensionality, simultaneity and unpredictability (Huberman, 1978, cited in Fullan, 1982). It is a context in which the self is constantly at risk. For example, confrontation with difficult pupils diminishes teachers' sense of efficacy (Webb and Ashton, 1987) and, by implication, their self-esteem. It is not surprising, therefore, that teachers expend considerable energy in the classroom attempting to minimize confrontational situations. The need to preserve a sense of self is, understandably, a strong determinant in the way teachers behave. The adherence to tried and tested strategies offers them a degree of reassuring stability and control.

The culture which permeates schools provides the normative beliefs and values through which individuals construct a sense of reality and a sense of self. Substantive change is inherently destabilizing because it challenges these largely taken-for-granted structures of meaning and, by implication, threatens the professional identities of teachers. Change also affects their career opportunities and aspirations and may undermine their ideological commitments. The more radical the change the greater the degree of destabilization.

From a biographical perspective, resistance to change can be explained as a psychological reaction to this loss of meaning. Marris (1974, p. 8) claims that 'there is a deep-seated impulse in all of us to defend the validity of what we have learned, for without it we would be helpless'. This he describes as 'the conservative impulse'. Any event that brings about a change in personal identity involves feelings of loss, anxiety and conflict. The effect is akin to grieving which Marris describes as 'the psychological process of adjustment to loss' (op.cit., p. 4).

A similar theme is evident in the work of Schon (1971). He claims that there is within us a strong and deep belief in the stable state; 'belief in the unchangeability, the constancy of central aspects of our lives, or belief that we can attain such a constancy' (op.cit., p. 9). Periods of change threaten central elements of the self, creating feelings of uncertainty and anguish. The degree of threat depends on its connection to self-identity.

Marris's work brings to the fore the psychological processes through which individuals make sense of the world; in short, how they learn. He resists the temptation to locate his ideas in any particular psychological theory although he does acknowledge the influence of Piaget. His own work, he states, 'is concerned with the consequences for mature adults of experiences they cannot readily assimilate to the structures of interpretation they have developed' (op.cit., p. 9), but with more emphasis placed 'on the part emotional attachment plays on the consolidation of these structures, and the parallel development of social structures to protect them' (ibid.).

Marris's work provides a useful framework for re-examining and, possibly, reinterpreting the change literature. Innovations that are consistent with the belief systems of teachers are readily assimilated into their prevailing 'structures of interpretation'. More radical innovations involve a loss of meaning which triggers 'the conservative impulse' and leads to 'grieving'. Therefore, 'teachers resist changes that do not make sense to them' (Heckman, 1987, p. 67). Research seems to support this interpretation. Innovations are often construed in familiar terms by practitioners and assimilated into their prevailing structures of meaning, rather than being allowed to pose a fundamental challenge to them. Olson, in reviewing his research on the Schools Council Integrated Science Project, confirms this. He claims that teachers

> made sense of the project by finding in the project what looked like familiar elements. They took these seemingly familiar events and used them in familiar ways. In other words the new system was stuck back together to look like the old. . . . familiar constructs were used in order to translate the project elements into a workable teaching scheme.
>
> (Olson, 1980, p. 6)

In Sarason's (1982) terms, the innovations had been assimilated into the existing 'programmatic and behavioral regularities' of the school culture.

In recent years increasing attention has been given to the phenomenon of teacher stress. The occupational stress of teaching is described by Kyriacou (1987, p. 146) as 'the experience . . . of unpleasant emotions, such as tension, frustration, anxiety, anger and depression, resulting from aspects of work as a teacher'. These emotions, similar to those experienced during the grieving process as identified by Marris (1974), are debilitating to human growth and, by implication, constitute a formidable barrier to change. Lauer and Lauer (1973) provide an interesting analysis of the relationship between change and stress. Following Shibutani (1961), they contend that 'the definition of the situation, the self-concept and the reference group are the social psychological bases for human behaviour' (p. 522). For the teacher the unpredictability of the reference group, that is 'the audience before which he [*sic*] tries to maintain his self-respect' (ibid.), could be seen as a particular source of stress. According to Lauer and Lauer, the main cause of stress is not change *per se* but the rate and kind of change. Rapid change generates greater stress in that it undermines the psychological bases of behaviour. However, stress is reduced if the change is perceived by those it affects as controllable and desirable. Other research seems to support this claim. Evidence indicates that teachers who perceive the 'locus of control' in their lives as external experience more stress (Kyriacou, 1987).

The implications of this are far reaching. In order to minimize the stress on teachers it is essential that they are given greater control over the pace and direction of change. Currently in Britain the reverse is happening. Throughout the 1980s teachers were confronted with a barrage of policy initiatives designed to bring about significant, but often contradictory, changes in the process of schooling. Even so, they retained some ownership of and control over these changes. This is no longer the case. Through the implementation of the National Curriculum, in accordance with the 1988 Education Reform Act, the 'locus of control' has shifted substantially away from practitioners. Teachers are now required to 'deliver' a centrally determined curriculum and to assess pupils in relation to criteria they had no say in formulating, using tests they have little say in devising. Moreover, schools are expected to respond rapidly and unquestioningly to every idiosyncratic change in government policy. The conditions under which teachers now practise are, therefore, highly inductive of stress. Unfortunately, the tendency is to address the problem of stress in terms of symptoms rather than causes. There is an inherent danger that teachers, and those who support them professionally, may too readily and too uncritically strive to make centrally prescribed policies 'work', regardless of the educational merits, in order to regain some control over their professional lives.

Goodson (1991) argues that attempts to understand and promote change from a biographical perspective have focused too narrowly on the classroom practice of teachers. He argues on strategic and substantive grounds for 'a broadening of focus to allow detailed scrutiny of the teacher's life and work' (op.cit., p. 39). There is a respectable and growing body of research available on teachers' lives and careers (Sikes, Measor and Woods, 1985; Ball and Goodson, 1989; Goodson, 1991; Goodson and Walker, 1991) as told by the teachers themselves. This work provides a framework for examining the responses of teachers to change within the wider context of their personal and professional lives. Even so, most of this research has been conducted from a researcher's perspective within an interpretative research paradigm. Accounts of teachers' careers and lives have been generated primarily in the interest of researchers rather than as a vehicle for the professional development of teachers. Thus, while researchers acknowledge the need to give teachers a voice, they do so by casting them as the objects of their research. This is not to deny the value of this research but to recognize its limitations in promoting educational change. Recent approaches to this research, however, are more collaborative and focus explicitly on eliciting from teachers accounts of their lives and practices as an integral part of professional development programmes. The work of Holly (1991), for example, demonstrates the efficacy of journal writing in helping teachers to reflect critically and systematically upon their practice, thereby reconceptualizing and changing it, and to develop deeper insights into their existential selves.

Research, using life history method, suggests that during their career cycle teachers pass through a number of discrete stages or phases, characterized by different attitudes, perceptions, concerns, expectations, commitments, etc. Sikes (1985), following Levinson, identifies a number of age-group phases. Similarly, Measor (1985) identifies a number of 'intrinsic critical phases' within the natural progression of the teachers' careers. Huberman (1988) examines the career cycle of teachers more explicitly in relation to attempts at school improvement. His research, based on an analysis of interviews conducted with 160 Swiss teachers, implies that teachers' careers consist of a number of identifiable phases or stages which are passed through sequentially. He argues that within the total context of a teacher's career, innovations are but fleeting moments in time. And he points out the significance of this: 'large-scale innovations . . . constitute a few brief episodes in a professional and personal biography, one of several events in a life phase, and are rooted in a biography that makes them momentous or trivial according to the issues and energy they activate at the moment of their occurrence' (op.cit., p. 120). His research demonstrates that from phase to phase the commitment of teachers to innovation varies. In general, having consolidated their basic repertoires teachers enter a phase where the willingness and energy to innovate is at its strongest. At the latter stage of a career teachers may enter a phase characterized by 'a pulling back, a narrowing of interests, a diminution of the energy available for collective innovations' (op.cit., p. 130). The reasons for this vary. For some it represents a 'natural' refocusing, for others 'disenchantment' through the failure of past innovations. And a further group had resisted innovation in the past and, in their remaining years, could derive some satisfaction from activities not yet corrupted. The implication of Huberman's findings, and of career cycle research in general, is clear. If a change initiative is 'out of phase' with an individual's career it is likely to be either ignored or resisted.

From a biographical perspective change is contingent upon the professional development of individual practitioners carried out within the context of their wider psychological needs; their hopes, fears, aspirations, etc. The success of an innovation is dependent upon the material and psychological support that individuals and groups are given in constructing new sets of meaning. Innovation is synonymous with learning, and learning is often a painful process. It involves, indeed requires, a certain level of dissonance. The extent to which the dissonance which accompanies change is creative or destructive depends on how it is perceived and experienced by individuals. For effective learning to take place teachers need to feel 'in control of change' rather than to feel 'controlled by change'. In the words of Rudduck (1988, p. 210), 'If we are interested in substantial change, we may need to find structures and resources to help teachers to re-examine their purposes . . . slough off the sediment of socialization, and feel more in control of their professional purposes and direction'.

It is important to realize that the structures of meaning through which teachers interpret their work are not idiosyncratic; they are social constructions mediated through the occupational cultures and discourses within which teachers' practices are located. These in turn are located within and sustained by wider social, political and cultural structures and discourses. It is these structures that we will now examine.

## The structural perspective

The structural perspective has a long history but has undergone numerous revisions and additions over time. Central to this perspective is the assumption that the process of schooling is embedded in, and a reflection of, wider economic, social and political structures. One view sees education as the hegemonous means by which these structures are legitimated and 'reproduced' within capitalist modes of production. Within this view there is an element of structural determinism which denies or minimizes the possibility of human agency. However, the structures that impinge on the work of teachers operate at a number of levels and in different ways. At the macro level there are those social, economic, and political structures that are part of Western industrialized society itself. These find their most explicit expression in the educational policies of national or state governments. During the 1980s and continuing into the 1990s, Britain has witnessed a marked swing to the right of the political spectrum in both social and educational policy-making. This appears to be consistent with a general trend within Western capitalist societies as they endeavour to readjust to the demands of an emerging post-industrial social and economic order. Across the Western world political parties, conservative and socialist alike, are now defining education primarily in terms of producing an 'educated' and flexible workforce through the inculcation in young people of those skills and dispositions which are perceived to be necessary in order for them to respond to post-Fordian modes of production and consumption. Central to these policies are discourses which objectify the human subject as producer and consumer and reduce education to a marketable commodity.

Drawing on the social theory of Habermas, Hargreaves (1989) offers an interesting macrostructural interpretation of educational change in Britain over the last forty years. He claims that change during this period can be explained in terms of three educational crises which correspond closely to three social crises of the modern capitalist state, as identified by Habermas (1976). These three educational crises are of 'administration and reorganization', 'curriculum and belief' and 'motivation and assessment', corresponding to the social crises of 'rationality', 'legitimation' and 'motivation', respectively.

According to Hargreaves, the period from the late 1950s to the late 1970s was a period of optimism about expanding opportunity and social improvement in relation to post-war economic reconstruction, underpinned by a considerable degree of social and political consensus. However, there was a perceived lack of rationality between this optimism and educational provision. Concerns were expressed regarding the 'wastage of ability' and the 'hidden pool of talent'. The response to this crisis was administrative and concentrated on making education more accessible to all. It found expression in policies such as the expansion of higher education, the raising of the school leaving age and comprehensivization.

The mid-1970s to the early 1980s was a period of economic decline, perpetrating a crisis of belief in the legitimacy of society's basic institutions. In education the quality of schooling itself was questioned, setting in motion 'a re-examination of its basic purposes and processes' (op.cit., p. 106). The content of the curriculum was no longer seen as a solely professional matter but as one to be contested in the public arena. There was a marked shift in policy-making from questions of educational access to questions of curriculum entitlement. The outcome of this shift is well documented and need not be repeated here. Suffice to say it found its ultimate manifestation in the imposition on schools of the National Curriculum.

The early 1980s presaged the onset of a crisis of motivation brought about by increasing disillusionment during a period of rising unemployment. This itself was a consequence of macrostructural changes in the economy, particularly in relation to the decline of its manufacturing base. This crisis led to the implementation of a range of assessment policies designed to increase the motivation of pupils. These included GCSE (General Certificate of Secondary Education), CPVE (Certificate of Pre-Vocational Education), profiling, and records of achievement (RoA).

At the level of the school and the classroom – what Ball (1987) terms the meso level – another set of structures, over which teachers have limited control, comes into play. And, it could be argued, these structures themselves are structurally determined. They include the implementation of national and local government policies, resources, group sizes, pupil and parent expectations, wider social expectations, including those related to employment, and examination requirements. Further constraints are imposed by the kind, length and quality of initial and in-service education. Teachers often give the impression that from their perspective the major structural constraint on their work is that of time. Teachers, then, do not operate as free agents but within the constraints imposed by these structures. The degree of freedom that teachers can exercise in the school and classroom is not necessarily determined by the structures themselves but by how they are perceived by the teachers. And these perceptions in turn are ideologically structured. What is a frustrating constraint for one teacher is a golden opportunity for another.

The relationship between structure and agency is complex and has been the focus of a long-standing academic debate. It is not our intention to rehearse that debate here. However, we consider that a recognition of these structures, and an appreciation of the ways teachers respond to them, is imperative to an understanding of the process of change. Too often failure to bring about change is laid, uncritically and unfairly, at the teacher's door. It alerts us also to the dangers of accepting too readily over-deterministic explanations of teacher behaviour. For example, it has been argued (Flinders, 1988;

Hargreaves, 1990a) that the individualistic tendencies of teachers may not be a pathological response to the uncertainties of their profession – as is frequently assumed – but an 'adaptive strategy [which] protects the time and energy required to meet immediate instructional demands' (Flinders, op.cit., p. 25). Following Flinders, Hargreaves takes a similar line and suggests that teacher individualism could be explained as 'a rational economizing of effort and ordering of priorities in a highly pressed and constraining working environment' (Hargreaves, 1990a, p. 9).

Despite the constraints imposed by structures beyond their immediate control, teachers in Britain until recently enjoyed a level of autonomy not shared by their American and continental European counterparts. This of course has now changed. Giltin (1987) provides a salutary account of the effect that mandated curricula and compulsory testing have had on teacher behaviour in the USA. These structures are often manifested in a 'rationalized curriculum form' of sequential behavioural objectives such as GEMS (goal-based educational management system) and IGE (individually guided education). In Giltin's view, this kind of structure 'makes it necessary for teachers to spend a great deal of their time using technical skills: skills which give teachers the control and precision necessary efficiently to deliver bits of information to students and increase test scores' (p. 112). Thus, teachers develop a repertoire of narrow technical skills which, when used often enough, become habitual and 'assume a greater place within the teaching role' (ibid.). The lessons from this are clear and do not need to be spelt out by us.

Hargreaves (1989) highlights the difficulty of examining change from a single perspective. He agrees with the widespread view that the dominant culture of teaching seriously inhibits curriculum change. Moreover, he claims that of three widely adopted strategies of change two ignore, shore up or reinforce this culture thus frustrating the very change that they intend to promote. The first, 'cultural interruption', he defines as 'a process designed to develop, refine and transform the language and categories in which teachers think about their work' (p. 57). It endeavours to provide practitioners with new insights and understandings about the process of schooling. Individually pursued academic award-bearing courses represent the traditional version of this strategy. These Hargreaves considers to be largely ineffective because they do not mesh easily with the daily practical concerns of teaching. School-centred innovation represents a more promising alternative of this strategy. But, Hargreaves argues,

Given what we know about the culture of teaching . . . the use of teachers' present experience as the mainstay of explanations of classroom practice raises serious doubts about whether it will be possible to move beyond the bounds of existing practice to construct critical and collective revisions of the nature of teaching, still less to develop school-wide, state-wide or nation-wide policies of change.

(Hargreaves, op.cit., p. 58–9)

It has to be acknowledged that school-centred innovation often amounts to little more than a collective pooling of ignorance. However, Hargreaves in his analysis seems to ignore the possibility of research-oriented forms of school-centred innovation – as represented by collaborative action research – enabling teachers through systematic and critical reflection to consciously question the validity of present experience as the basis of their explanatory frameworks and, as a consequence, developing new ways of thinking and acting.

According to Hargreaves, the second change strategy responsible for sustaining the culture of teaching is 'structural reinforcement'. He claims that in Britain over the last few years this has operated in three ways: first, through the imposition of an academic subject-based curriculum; second, through an intensification of pressures and constraint upon the work of teachers which ties them more closely to the immediacy of the classroom; and third, through a reduction in in-service opportunities for extended reflection in exchange for short-term programmes of non-reflective training designed to equip teachers for the efficient delivery of policies determined elsewhere (op.cit., p. 62). Other examples of structural reinforcement, not cited by Hargreaves, are not too difficult to find. It is clearly evident in the criteria for initial education laid down by the Council for Accreditation of Teacher Education (CATE). Current changes in teacher education – the licensed teachers scheme and proposals for apprenticeship models of training – and the low-level 'instruction manual' publications emanating from the National Curriculum Council (NCC) and the School Examinations and Assessment Council (SEAC) are further examples.

Hargreaves concludes by arguing that attempts to transform the culture of teaching through the processes of cultural redefinition are unlikely to be successful unless they are linked with policies directed towards changing the existing material structures within which teaching is located. He makes a number of recommendations, the most far-reaching being 'the redefinition of worthwhile knowledge and cultural capital for all' (op.cit., p. 68).

While accepting the main thrust of Hargreaves's analysis and supporting the recommendations he makes, we wish to highlight certain inherent difficulties. The analysis over-homogenizes the culture of teaching, ignores the micropolitics of schools, contrary to his more recent work (Hargreaves, 1990a, 1990b), and gives little attention to the possibility of schools being sites of resistance and struggle. It fails to acknowledge the degree to which structural reinforcement has been welcomed and supported by powerful interests within the profession. For example, from the moment the idea was first mooted, the geographical establishment in general and the Geographical Association in particular supported the introduction of a National Curriculum and set about openly courting policy-makers at the highest level in order to ensure that geography was established as a constituent subject. As Goodlad (1987a, p. 211), using an ecological metaphor, puts it, 'the pollutants upstream may be the result of the misguided efforts of a subunit of the ecosystem rather than the work of a foreign saboteur'.

Finally, and perhaps most crucially, there is little evidence to suggest that the kinds of structural redefinitions advocated by Hargreaves have in the past resulted in any significant change in the culture of teaching. Structural changes such as comprehensivization, the introduction of the Certificate of Secondary Education (CSE), mixed ability teaching, subject integration, open plan classrooms, etc. provided the material and ideological base for a reconceptualization of education. What is of interest is the way the culture of teaching has been able to absorb, accommodate and survive, relatively unscathed, these quite significant structural changes. Perhaps the most satisfactory explanation for this resilience to change is to be found not in the culture of teaching but in the micropolitics of schooling.

Attempts by the government in the United Kingdom to reinforce or, more accurately perhaps, reconstruct certain structural features of the educational system are legitimated and supported by what Ball (1990) describes as 'discourses of derision'. The legitimation of discourse is a central theme in our analysis of change and will be analysed in depth in Chapter 5. Such an analysis is important because discursive practices impose constraints on the possibilities of thought and action and, by implication, the possibilities of change. Furthermore, it alerts us to what could be said but remains unsaid for reasons of ignorance or political expediency.

Allied to discourses of derision, and equally distorting, are discourses whereby the events of past eras are romanticized or, in the extreme, mythologized; what could, perhaps, be called discourses of illusion. These discourses are constructed at both ends of the educational spectrum. Traditionalists yearn for a return to a golden age of standards, Shakespeare and high culture. Progressivists mourn the loss of an age of innovation, child-centred practices and teacher autonomy. It is doubtful whether either ever really existed.

A number of theorists have examined change from an ecological perspective, notably Goodlad (1987a). The ecological perspective shares many of the assumptions of the structural and cultural perspectives but attempts to resolve some of the deficiencies inherent in these. It also highlights the interdependence of the structural and cultural dimensions of change. From this perspective, teachers' reaction to change proposals 'is seen as an outgrowth of efforts to meet environmental demands imposed by the distinctive ecology of the classroom' (Doyle and Ponder, 1977, p. 5). Their behaviour therefore represents 'a set of adaptive responses which have utility in negotiating classroom contingencies' (ibid.). By seeing teachers' responses to structural constraints as adaptive rather than determined, it envisages a greater degree of human agency in the process of change.

Perhaps the most powerful and pervasive structures that impinge on the work of teachers and influence the extent and direction of curriculum change are those of curriculum and assessment. As we have already seen, the culture of teaching and teachers' occupational identities derive from these structures, and it is in relation to and through these structures that the micropolitics of schools are often played out. It is to a closer examination of these structures that we now turn.

## The sociohistorical perspective

In recent years, following the seminal work of Ivor Goodson (1981, 1983), considerable attention has been directed towards an examination of curriculum from a sociohistorical perspective. This perspective offers a useful framework for analysing and interpreting the process of curriculum change. Expressed simply, it represents an attempt to understand 'where subjects came from and why they were as they were' (Goodson, 1987, p. viii). His work focuses primarily on the written or preactive curriculum: he makes no attempt to examine curriculum 'in practice' or 'as practice'. This does not imply that he considers this dimension of curriculum as unimportant. On the contrary, he argues that any analysis of curriculum 'as practice' is meaningless without an understanding of 'the preactive definitions' and 'antecedent structures' (Goodson 1988) within which that practice is located. In short, our understanding of curriculum practice is enhanced through an examination of its historical and social construction. His work is an explicit attempt to make good a deficiency in curriculum research and analysis as described by Young (1971, p. 24): 'We have virtually no theoretical perspective or research to suggest explanations of how curricula, which are no less social inventions than political parties or new towns, arise, persist and change and what the social interests and values involved might be'.

Indeed, Goodson acknowledges that the genesis of his work is in the sociology of knowledge as propounded by, among others, Young, Bernstein and Keddie (Young, 1971). Their central thesis is that the curriculum provides the means whereby dominant groups in society are able to maintain a position of power by exercising control over subordinate groups. In the oft-quoted words of Bernstein (1971, p. 47), 'How a society classifies, distributes, transmits and evaluates the educational knowledge it considers to be public, reflects both the distribution of power and the principle of social control'.

Goodson advocates caution in relation to this particular sociology of knowledge thesis. Who, he asks, are these dominant groups? He claims that historical studies pose questions concerning whose interest dominance serves. Does it serve, for example, the interests of professional groups or sociocultural dominant groups, or the interests of industrial and financial capital? Moreover, he claims that the process whereby the unspecified dominant groups exercise control over subordinate groups is not scrutinized. He highlights the dangers of generating macrosociological theories of knowledge without undertaking empirical studies of how disciplines and subjects have been constructed over time. His own analysis is centred on three working hypotheses:

(1) Subjects are not monolithic entities but shifting amalgamations of subgroups and traditions.
(2) In the process of establishing a school there is a tendency for subject-based subject groups to move from promoting pedagogic and utilitarian traditions towards the academic tradition.
(3) In case studies much of the curriculum debate can be interpreted in terms of conflict between subjects over status resources and territory.

These hypotheses provided the basis for Goodson's (1981) own sociohistorical analysis of geography as an academic discipline and school subject and have been utilized by a number of researchers undertaking similar analyses in other areas of the curriculum (Goodson and Ball, 1984; Goodson, 1985). They provide a framework for researching and analysing the various elements of the curriculum and how these elements interrelate both in their current manifestations and over time. Consequently, sociohistorical analyses have made a significant contribution to curriculum studies and offer important insights into the process of change. These analyses help explain the persistence of a monolithic academic subject-based curriculum against which the hopes of many innovations have been dashed. They also offer an explanation of the somewhat ambivalent response of the educational establishment to the National Curriculum.

Curriculum histories show that academic subject communities are living cultures through which many teachers construct and express their occupational and personal identities. When a teacher says 'I'm a geographer' or 'I'm a historian' more is implied than a statement about the subject he/she teaches. It is a reiteration of allegiance to a collective learning community which confers upon its members a sense of competence and status and reinforces in an individual a particular view of his/her occupational and existential self.

Moreover, as we have already noted, subjects are closely related to the material base of teachers' occupational and personal lives; their social standings and career prospects are closely linked to the fortunes of their subject. It is not surprising, therefore, that subject subcultures are often the source of micropolitical rivalries and conflicts. The school curriculum, as a sociohistorical construct, is inherently political and the promotion of one area will involve campaigning against the interests of others. Hence Goodson's (1987, p. 3) assertion that 'much of the curriculum debate can be interpreted in terms of conflicts between subjects over status, resources and territory'. Note the reaction of the geographical establishment to the National Curriculum Science Statutory Orders which were perceived to infringe on its territory. Storm (1989a, p. 13), defending the interests of geography, alludes to the 'intellectually megalomaniacal science proposals' and to the 'gargantuan claim of science to encompass just about everything' (Storm, 1989b, p. 103).

Embedded in subject hierarchies are social relationships between people that constitute powerful determinants of the possibility of change. Young (1971, p. 34) points out that 'as we assume some social relations associated with any curriculum . . . changes will be resisted in so far as they are perceived to undermine the values, relative power and privileges of the dominant group involved'. Thus, the study of curriculum change from a sociohistorical perspective furnishes important understandings concerning the micropolitics of schools.

Inter-subject contestations are not confined to schools. They are fought on a number of levels and sites. School subjects are supported by powerful subject associations whose main concern is to advance the interests of the subjects they represent rather than education as a whole. Once a subject has established a firm footing in the curriculum, it is difficult to dislodge for, as Dewey (1916, p. 228) points out, 'no fortified and protected interest readily surrenders any monopoly it may possess'. Therefore, certain subjects persist in the curriculum not because of their intrinsic qualities but because of the political power and material resources they have at their disposal.

Nor should intra-subject conflicts be ignored in examining the curriculum from a sociohistorical perspective. On the contrary, this is a central focus of Goodson's work. The current 'empathy' debate in history serves to illustrate this point (a debate, moreover, that has become increasingly political). Similar debates are found in other areas of the curriculum. During the last thirty years there has been a concerted effort to recast geography, at all levels of study, as a law-seeking discipline, utilizing the principles and methods of positive science (Edwards, 1991). This is perceived as the final 'coming of age' for geography as an academic discipline. But it has been achieved at the expense of those radical and humanistic approaches to geography associated with critical and phenomenological/existential research paradigms; approaches, ironically, which have far greater potential for incorporating the learners' own experiences, values and perceptions into the educational process (Edwards, op.cit.).

# SUMMARY AND CONCLUSIONS

This chapter has explored a number of theoretical perspectives on curriculum change which have emerged from studies of the many attempts which have been made to change the curriculum in recent years.

That exploration has revealed, first, the inadequacies of some, perhaps all, of the strategies which have been adopted to bring about such change. In particular, it has highlighted the difficulties of effecting change from outside the school. For the attempt to do this takes no account of the factors, some of them unique, within every school which will act as barriers to genuine change if our strategies and mechanisms do not fully and properly allow for them.

Second, the chapter considered some of the theoretical perspectives which have emerged from studies of the realities of change within individual institutions or, rather, the detailed realities of the sources of resistance to change which have been identified as offering explanations of the ineffectiveness of many attempts at change and as factors which must be taken into account if planned change is to 'take' in a school. The obvious importance of these perspectives reinforces the claim we made at the beginning of the chapter that without a full appreciation of these emergent theories, curriculum change cannot be planned with any hope of real success. It is also further evidence of our continuing claim that a sound theoretical base is needed for sound practice in all areas of educational planning.

# 3

# NATIONAL AGENCIES
# AND CURRICULUM CHANGE

The major message of Chapter 1 was that, if we take a 'post-modern' view of change as transformative rather than as incremental or accumulative, if we reject any metaphysical notion of permanence or stability and thus of development as leading on towards perfection, we must see and plan the curriculum in such a way as to facilitate the process of change, and we must devise structures or strategies which will both permit and support such change within the curriculum itself.

Chapter 2 outlined some of the theoretical perspectives which have been developed as a basis not only for analysing and understanding educational change but also as a framework for planning such change and devising strategies for bringing it about.

One such strategy has been the establishment of national bodies to promote curriculum change. This chapter sets out to examine this strategy and, in particular, the different forms it has taken. That examination will in turn provide the base from which Chapter 4 will consider other mechanisms for change, mechanisms of a local, even individual, school-based form, most, if not all, of which have resulted from the experience of these attempts at change on a national scale.

There are two ways in which such national agencies can or may have an impact on the curriculum and bring about curriculum change. First, the agency may be established expressly to effect change in the school curriculum. Second, however, the change may be a result of the unintended influences of an agency set up not with the intention of prompting curriculum change but to fulfil some other purpose – to assess pupil performance, for example, or to evaluate the effectiveness of schools.

A second major distinction which we must note at the outset of our discussion of the role of national agencies in curriculum change is that between those agencies which have set out to *influence* curriculum change, to persuade teachers of the desirability of certain kinds of change, and those which have been created to *impose* certain forms of change and to exercise direct control over the curriculum.

These two factors are the main criteria by which we have distinguished in this chapter between the different kinds of national agency which have exercised an influence on the curriculum of schools in the United Kingdom during the last two or three decades. The chapter is therefore divided into three sections. First, it examines the work of those agencies, most notably the Schools Council, which were established with the prime purpose of promoting curriculum change. Second, it explores the impact of national bodies which, while not set up with the express intention of changing the curriculum, have nevertheless had an impact on it. This section will be concerned especially with the work of the Assessment of Performance Unit (APU), but it will also consider the influences of the examination boards on the curriculum of the secondary school. Finally, it examines the work of those bodies, particularly the National Curriculum Council (NCC), which have been set up to manage the compulsory curriculum change which has been imposed upon all schools in the maintained sector by the 1988 Education Reform Act and the National Curriculum which that Act has brought with it.

We will thus be considering, first, deliberate attempts to influence and change the curriculum through research, development and the dissemination of ideas; second, national agencies which, while not specifically concerned with the curriculum as such, have by their activities influenced it; and, finally, current attempts not merely to influence the curriculum and/or to attempt to promote and support curriculum change and development, but to impose change, to implement government policies and to exercise direct curriculum control.

First, then, let us look at the work of those agencies which have been created to support curriculum change and development through research and the dissemination of ideas, and especially the work of the Schools Council.

## AGENCIES FOR SUPPORTING CURRICULUM CHANGE AND DEVELOPMENT

Before we look at the work of such agencies, we should remind ourselves of a point which was made in Chapter 2 and which will be expanded in Chapter 5. There is a tendency among those who would have us adopt their policies to create, to legitimate, new forms of discourse and, in doing so, to attempt to oust older forms, especially by dubbing them 'outmoded' or 'old hat'. We also claimed in Chapter 2 that, in the interests of the continuation of a free and open debate about educational policy, current forms of discourse need to be seen for what they are and the insights of earlier debates maintained.

Although agencies for research, development and the dissemination of ideas about the curriculum, such as the Schools Council, no longer exist, but have been replaced by agencies with a much more directive, and indeed political, role, and although the curriculum debate which the work of these agencies fuelled has given way in most places to a much more limited and limiting form of discourse, it would be a serious mistake for us to view any exploration of their work as if it were merely a historical exercise. The insights gained from that work have an important part to play in any rational approach to educational planning or in any properly intellectual debate about the school curriculum. Indeed, it has been claimed, with some justification, that the refusal to make use of those insights is one of the major reasons for the serious flaws that can be seen in the National Curriculum (Kelly, 1990).

The work of these agencies reflects an era when professionals were, rightly or wrongly, more in control of educational practice than they are today, and when curriculum development, as a smooth transition from one form to another, was being actively explored both in professional practice and theory. It was the time of the birth of curriculum study, of the theoretical examination of the professional practice of teachers, what Lawrence Stenhouse (1980) subsequently called the curriculum development movement. An examination of this, while it involves looking back in the historical sense, in fact is a process of looking forward, in the sense that, compared with the way curriculum change is perceived in the present climate, it is light-years ahead in ideas and in its implications for professional practice.

Hence, the consideration of the work of the Schools Council which follows is a descriptive case study of a period when some fascinating issues arose related to curriculum development, certainly in the United Kingdom but also in the USA and the other English-speaking countries, although not so much in Europe, a period which also provided us with the essence of curriculum theory. It is thus a prime example of curriculum development, and it also reflects an era when the school curriculum, and the curriculum debate too, were, not totally, though much more than today, under the control of professional teachers.

It is important to note that at the time when it was happening much of this work did not reach or touch the consciousness of many practising teachers. Change that is development – in ideas, in theory and in professional practice – takes time to take root and become part of the culture. What is of concern about the change which schools are experiencing at present is that it fits in with the existing culture, because its underlying assumptions are dated, they are 'old-hat', they have been around since at least the beginning of the century, they reflect that Newtonian paradigm we suggested in Chapter 1 has been transcended in every other sphere, and it is thus easy for teachers to take on. The ideas that emerged from the work of the Schools Council, on the other hand, were innovatory in a genuine sense; they were developments in our thinking about education and curriculum as well as in our professional practice.

These are ideas, then, which need to be preserved in preparation for the next era. And there are certainly signs in American theory and practice, which is usually about 15 years ahead of that in the United Kingdom, that such a new era is opening up (Malkus, Feldman and Gardner, 1988), that there they are emerging from the traumas currently endured by education in the UK, and that they are doing so by coming up with ideas that are developments of some of the insights that arose from the life and the work of the Schools Council.

## The Schools Council (1964–1983)

The Schools Council was a funding institution, charged with promoting change and development in schools. Its focus and form were professional. It was not the only funding agency, so that all sources of funding did not disappear with its demise. Although similar organizations, such as the Social Science Research Council (SSRC), also a large sponsor of educational research, subsequently disappeared or at least were replaced, the National Foundation for Educational Research (NFER), another large sponsor, is still in existence, and very much involved in the current exercise of developing Standard Assessment Tasks (SATs). Indeed, the Department of Education and Science (DES) itself was, throughout the life of the Schools Council, a much larger sponsor of educational research than the council itself ever was, and is still the major funding body in the United Kingdom.

As a funding body, the Schools Council's influence on the projects and development work it sponsored was not as direct as is sometimes assumed. Much of the responsibility for curriculum development was delegated to the project teams which were located largely in those institutions of higher education which had attracted sponsorship for research from the council. The council did, of course, adopt a supervisory role in relation to each of its projects, but there is little evidence of co-ordination between projects or, indeed, between the council's sponsoring committees.

The Schools Council was thus one of several sources of funding for educational research; its own funding came partly from central government, partly from local education authorities and partly (a small proportion) from independent sources. It is of some significance, however, that the two funding bodies which were discontinued in the 1980s were those which were, politically speaking, largely independent. And those which might have been independent, the institutions of higher education, have during that decade worked under increasing constraints, since, with the demise of these two bodies, funding has become much harder to attract and has not been without its political strings, in relation to both the areas of research and development which have been funded and the kinds of research and development which have been permitted, as we shall see in subsequent sections of this chapter. We are thus left in the present era with funding bodies which are nationally, centrally and politically controlled, especially the DES and the NFER. Thus the climate of national curriculum research, development and change has altered quite significantly, and a large proportion of professional independence has been lost. In contrast, when the Schools Council was established, the climate was one of innovation and optimism.

The *form* of any national agency for curriculum change and development, therefore, is important, not least because it provides us with a clue as to the bias of interest which that agency is likely to reveal. It is certainly true that the work of the Schools Council was heavily biased by professional interests. This proved to be one of its weaknesses as well as one of its strengths. The form of a national agency is also important in defining the impact it will have on the curriculum in relation to its bias, whether this be a professional/research bias, a profit-making bias or a political bias. Currently, in the United Kingdom, the bias is political, with some elements of profit-making, especially apparent in the activities of some of the publishing houses. Thus it becomes important to identify the underlying values and assumptions of any national body concerned with curriculum change and development.

A second introductory point to be made is that in the United

Kingdom the attitude to research and development is an important factor. In comparison to the USA, for example, where educational research is much more utopian in style and where, if a problem is recognized, a solution is much more likely to be sought through research, the approach in the United Kingdom is much more piece-meal. This means, on the one hand, that it has been more difficult to exercise control over the curriculum in the United Kingdom. On the other hand, it also means that development itself has been fragmented and haphazard.

There is also in the United Kingdom a fundamental suspicion of research. Teachers have tended to resist research and to be dismissive of it. This is a characteristic not only of teachers but of our culture generally. Nancy Trenaman, for example, comments on this charac-teristic in her review of the submissions and criticisms that she received from professionals, politicians and lay people about the Schools Council's work, and she notes that 'I personally found the anti-intellectual flavour of some of the discussions in the meetings that I attended tiresome and unnecessary: certainly I never heard the word "academic" used save in a pejorative sense' (DES, 1981, p. 33). To attempt to promote change when such attitudes are widespread presents serious problems for research and development in education.

On the other hand, this scepticism has also led to some interesting issues being raised in relation to research. For example, in the USA, although they are more accepting of and optimistic about research, they are much less likely to question the style of it. As we shall see later, in the United Kingdom interesting questions have been raised about, for example, the scientific approach to research in education and whether such an approach is likely to yield valid results – a debate which is still going on.

The third point which must be made is that there are other bodies with an interest in and an influence on national research and devel-opment in education. Clearly there are the many political groups seeking to achieve their different goals through the schooling system. Second, there are the publishing houses which have an influence not only through publication of the research findings themselves but also, especially apparent in the current scene, through the publication of materials for teachers to use with their classes. Third, there are still the examination boards, which have made innovatory changes and are perhaps in a better position than most at present to preserve important areas of the curriculum. One might also cite parents here, but there are real doubts as to how far they are influential at a national level, especially at present, in spite of the political rhetoric of giving more power and choice to parents. Indeed, parents may have been more influential nationally in previous eras, such as that when the Schools Council was at its busiest and most active. It is perhaps also worth noting that the influence of the teachers' unions on educational research and development has been minimal, although there are now some indications that that influence may have begun to increase over the last few years. It is important to note, however, that even during the life of the Schools Council, there were other groups and agencies seeking to influence the curriculum and to promote change within it (Plaskow, 1985).

Fourth, it is worth explaining why the Schools Council has been chosen as a case study of a national agency for curriculum development. One reason is that, as was noted above, it was the largest such agency after the DES itself. It was the major independent agency of its time, and thus centre-stage for government criticism, of which it received much. It also faced a lot of criticism from the teaching profession itself, and from parents and educational journalists and commentators. It was thus a focus for the debate about educational change, both within the teaching profession and in society at large. It was also the first time in the history of education in the United Kingdom that there was an independent body to provide such a focus for this kind of national debate, the first time there was a focus other than the purely political. It thus put a spotlight on how educational research and development could occur. It was of course rather coy and reticent about its *research* role, reflecting those characteristics of both the teaching profession and our culture which we mentioned earlier. However, at the same time it did provide a mass of evidence, which is still available to us, about the nature of curriculum research and development. It is a major source of examples of curriculum development at both the local and the national levels. In reviewing the general legacy of the curriculum movement, Stenhouse highlights the importance of the products of the Schools Council's projects. He argues that it is the legacy of materials, handbooks and other artefacts that embody 'ideas of great power . . . and are the best outside source of ideas about pedagogy and knowledge for teachers who will approach them as critical professionals who perceive ideas not as threats to their own professional autonomy, but as supports for it' (Stenhouse, 1983a, p. 354). Produced in a time of plenty and optimism, he notes, these products and powerful ideas are of particular importance to reflective professionals during a time of gloom and recession. The Schools

Council has run its course and its 'complete works' are there for our perusal and consideration. Hence, one reason for examining its work in detail is that it is the largest complete example we have available to us of this kind of national agency.

A second major reason for elaborating on its work is that even the most cursory glance at that work reveals how far it highlighted many of the issues and problems associated with attempts at curriculum development and at the practical implementation of curriculum planning. Not only did it highlight these issues, it also offered considerable insights into them. For example, it drew our attention to issues related to assessment, to evaluation, to dissemination, to accountability, to the relationships of knowledge and skills in learning and to many others. In fact, any issue related to thoughtful reflection on curriculum development and practice can be found illuminated by some aspect of the council's work, identified in the practice and also theorized about by the project leaders and their teams.

A third reason for emphasizing its work is that it offers an interesting and important insight into the effects of centralization on education, insights which must raise doubts as to whether the present National Curriculum, as a rather crude attempt at centralized control of the curriculum, can or will actually work. The Schools Council's work sheds useful light on the reasons why it is difficult to make centralization of curriculum research and development work at the level of the school. And some of the general points which the Schools Council's work unearthed are relevant to any attempt at centralized control.

Finally, it is a major source of references on curriculum issues. The council's reports, working papers and bulletins evince a truly professional style, in so far as they take teachers seriously and attempt to promote a serious and penetrating professional dialogue. This provides a major contrast to the glossy, lightweight and condescending publications the profession now receives from the NCC, the Schools Examinations and Assessment Council (SEAC) and, indeed, from the DES itself: publications clearly designed, as we shall see in Chapter 5, to confine the curriculum debate within those parameters we referred to earlier. There are also the annual reports of its work as a whole which throw much light on issues related to the administration of a national agency. There is too the independent evaluation of its work as a national agency, the Trenaman Report (DES, 1981), which details the case for curriculum development through national initiatives but argues strongly against political control of such initiatives, a persuasive argument which has been ignored in the current era. Finally, as was seen in Chapter 2, there is the literature which has been generated by those who have commented on the work of the Schools Council or endeavoured to pursue in their own work the insights it offered and thus to develop curriculum theory as a continuing debate at a properly critical and analytical level.

First, then, let us fill in briefly some of the background detail of the council's early work. It emerged as a reaction against the attempt to establish central political control in the early 1960s, and was a direct result of the unhappiness expressed by the profession about the role of the Curriculum Study Group, a political body. It was thus the product of a professional optimism at a period when the teaching profession was perhaps at its most powerful. (That power was a result of the profession asserting itself over matters of pay and conditions of service rather than over curriculum matters as such. Nevertheless, it is quite clear that the politicians were not at that time prepared to take on the teachers.) Thus the Schools Council, with a majority of teachers on virtually all of its major committees, was established as a sort of compromise, and arose out of what seemed to be politically expedient at that time.

To this body was then entrusted responsibility for curriculum research and development and – a most important point – for the oversight of examinations. Not only, therefore, was it set up to replace the politically controlled Curriculum Study Group, it also took over from the Secondary Schools Examinations Council (SSEC) responsibility for examinations.

It is important to remember that there was no such thing as professional curriculum theory in the United Kingdom at that time. Behavioural theories of curriculum and instruction were being developed in the USA at the time, but, until the establishment of the Schools Council, professional theory in Britain consisted of philosophy, psychology and sociology – disciplines which are related to education but are not centrally educational. One significant aspect of the impact of this national agency under the professional control of teachers was that curriculum theory, a body of theoretical understanding to underpin the professional practice of teachers, began to emerge in its own right, not as derivative from other disciplines but arising from an intellectual confrontation of curriculum practice.

The Schools Council took over immediately those existing research projects which were conceived of as curriculum projects, such as those sponsored by the Nuffield Foundation, in areas such as science, mathematics and modern languages. And, through these projects, it took on what was very much the American model of curriculum research and development mentioned above. In doing so, it also took on a very traditional view of what curriculum is, a view not dissimilar to that endemic to the current National Curriculum. It set up a number of programmes, and committees to be responsible for these programmes, and these were mainly concerned with, and thus reflected, a secondary school view of the curriculum, a subject-focused view, all the work in the primary sector being placed under the aegis of one committee. There was only one subject committee as such, the English committee, but the organization of the work within committees makes it clear that the underlying concept of curriculum was very much a subject/content view. This even extended to the primary programme, perhaps most obviously through the projects in primary science. However, there is some evidence in this primary programme that attempts soon began to be made to address issues in a cross-curricular manner, and to take on, for example, some of the policy recommendations of the Plowden Committee (CACE, 1967). A lot of the Schools Council's work that related to compensatory education and its associated issues was directly linked to the Plowden Report's proposals and arose out of the research sponsored by the primary programme. In general, however, the council initially set itself up with a very traditional structure, dominated by thinking about the secondary school curriculum and, within that, sponsoring in the main projects related to school subjects.

The structure that was established at the beginning set the pattern for the first ten years. However, quite early in its life, and certainly during this first ten years, there was evidence within the council of unhappiness about this self-imposed structure. Most of the early working papers, for example, raised cross-curricular issues of a kind that were not being reached within the structure that had been established. A concern emerged, too, about a broader range of issues than those which arose within the traditional organization and division of schools. Attention was directed, for example, towards issues related to pre-school provision, and in the latter part of that ten-year period work was undertaken in the field of nursery education. In short, issues were arising which focused on the children themselves rather than merely on the content of their curriculum, and these began to be recognized as important issues in curriculum development. Projects were set up which were related to gifted children, for example, to travelling children, to disadvantaged children, to children with special educational needs and so on. Attention also began to be given to broad issues such as the relation of the school curriculum to industry, through projects in careers education, and to issues of school organization and its impact on the whole curriculum (Schools Council Link).

Although the Schools Council originally adopted this very rigid and traditional structure (not unlike that now established by the politicians through the National Curriculum), it soon began to realize how far its work was constrained by that structure and how important it was to seek a more flexible administrative context for its work.

A third point that should be noted is that, throughout its life, the council was concerned with evaluation and testing, and some of its most significant and penetrating work was in that field. Also, after only five years of its existence, one can see through the reports, newsletters and other publications that the council was becoming very concerned about the dissemination of ideas and of curriculum development. Certainly after the first ten years it was making explicit statements about its concern over this important area of the link between its research and development activities and their dissemination to teachers (Schools Council, 1975). It was also revealing a good deal of sensitivity to the fact that, despite all its efforts and investment in this respect, matters were not proceeding in a satisfactory professional manner.

Although the political attacks on the council would give the impression that these issues had never been addressed, it is certainly not fair to accuse it of being unconcerned, especially in the last nine years of its existence, about developing cross-curricular strategies and supporting teachers in developing good practice at the school level. Indeed, the restructuring in 1980 of its work into broad programmes, which included 'Helping Teachers' Professional Development' (Programme 2) and 'The Needs of Individual Pupils' (Programme 4), indicates the degree of its responsiveness to the real world of professional practice and curriculum change (Schools Council, 1980).

Let us now consider the major lessons to be learned from the experience of the Schools Council, many of which will be explored further in Chapter 4.

First, an immense amount was learned about models of curriculum planning. Within a period of twenty years there grew, purely through practical experience, an enormous dissatisfaction with the narrow behavioural model inherited through those early projects. Simply, this model did not work. It did not work educationally or even, in narrow terms, as a device for instilling knowledge. All attempts at producing 'teacher-proof' packages proved to be misconceived as teachers took what was offered and used it to suit their own individual classroom purposes and contexts; they 'cannibalized' everything. Some project directors found this objectionable and irritating, just as Skinner (1968) regarded the teacher as the inefficient factor in the educational process and expressed a preference for teaching machines, and just as some today are already blaming teachers for any failure to 'deliver' the prepackaged National Curriculum. Others, however, such as Alan Blyth (1974), recognized this phenomenon for what it was – evidence that this was not a satisfactory or effective way to plan or to attempt to change the curriculum, evidence that the teacher must be seen as central to the activity, along with the child, and that attempts to impose systems from outside will invariably fail.

Hence, there was first an awareness of the deficiencies of this simplistic model of curriculum planning, and, consequently, the development of some very sophisticated models to replace it: Stenhouse's notion of the teacher as researcher (1975), for example, the research model of curriculum development, developmental models of curriculum planning (Blenkin and Kelly, 1981, 1987a, 1987b) and so on. This was one debate, perhaps the best documented, which emerged from the work of the Schools Council.

A second issue that its work raised was that related to the 'politics of educational knowledge', power and educational knowledge, knowledge and social control. For it became the main catalyst of the ideas of Michael Young (1971), who illustrates most of the arguments he develops with examples from the council's work and relates this to the 'myth' of teacher autonomy, the too-ready legitimization of subjects into an institutional hierarchy by the establishment of this kind of national agency, and also the tendency of national agencies to relate 'types' of children and types of knowledge, thus depriving certain categories of children of access to certain kinds of knowledge and reinforcing social class and ethnic divisions rather than attempting to overcome them.

Again, to level this kind of charge at the Schools Council may be unfair. Its work certainly highlighted this kind of issue, but it is clear that it revised its structure and adjusted its policy after the first ten years or so of its existence precisely because of an awareness of this kind of problem. It no longer maintained that original committee structure; it no longer confined its activities to that traditional subject-based kind of sponsorship. And this was largely because its experience had raised in practice exactly the kinds of difficulty Young was identifying in theory. Furthermore, in its later work it is plain that the council was making proposals designed, in a very genuine sense, to promote education for all; this work started to offer clear evidence as to how, at a national level, we might set about achieving this. It might be argued, therefore, not that the council perpetuated the problems of knowledge and control but that its work again offered insights into those problems and led it to seek effective strategies for avoiding them and being constructively responsive to the notion of universal education. In other words, here again it can be seen as contributing to a continuing debate about fundamental educational issues, a debate which is not evident in current policies for the school curriculum.

A third interesting area of the council's influence is its work in relation to examinations and assessment. It is worth noting that in the current politically driven system there is a very uneasy relationship between the body responsible for the curriculum (NCC) and that established to oversee examinations and assessment (SEAC), one of the first steps taken by the DES in the creation of the present system having been to separate these two functions. Because it had responsibility for both, the Schools Council was able to say some very interesting things about a productive role for examinations and assessment within education, again in spite of the fact that many teachers were resistant to the idea of examinations having a positive role in curriculum development, seeing them as an inevitable constraint on their work and as inhibiting them from any attempt to change or develop the curriculum. This was not true of the Council's earlier work, which adopted a rather traditional view and seemed to be based on the assumption that it is sufficient to set up a separate committee to develop imaginative examinations. Again, however, after five or six years one can see, through the examination bulletins, a debate emerging about how to develop assessment procedures and examinations which actually promote curriculum development (Matthews and Leece, 1976). The examination boards, for example, through the work of curriculum projects sponsored by the council, began to change and develop the subjects for which they were responsible, the most notable example of this perhaps being the development which occurred in what subsequently came to be called Design and Technology, where the O- and A-level GCE examination strategies played a major part in changing the whole way in which that area of the curriculum was conceived and addressed in schools. It was the close links between the curriculum projects sponsored by the council and its responsibility for examinations which brought these aspects of educational planning together. Again it is apparent in current policies that the separation of them is leading to some very uneasy relationships between the newly created bodies, NCC and SEAC, and to consequential difficulties in practice, not to mention problems of the relationship of both bodies to the DES.

Hence, from the experience of the Schools Council, there arose a strong argument that curriculum development and pupil assessment need to be considered together, that developments in the one cannot occur without corresponding developments in the other. This was as apparent in relation to assessment in the early years of schooling as in public examinations at secondary level. For issues of assessment were addressed at all levels of the education system, and this embraced record-keeping systems and profiling as well as examinations. The concern throughout was with assessment related to curriculum development and not as something which could be planned and conducted in isolation from it.

A fourth area in which major lessons were there to be learned, was the area of dissemination, to which we referred earlier. Early projects showed clearly the limitations, indeed the failure, of RD&D models of change. It is worth noting here, however, that, as we shall see in greater detail in Chapter 4, in the last five or so years of its life the council developed, in response to some of the problems of dissemination it had encountered, some imaginative ways in which, as a national agency, it could reach the teachers in the schools and support curriculum development at a school-based level. Although it was being claimed by many at the time that effective curriculum development had to be school based, the work of the council in its final years gave evidence of the degree to which such school-based developments could be supported, and indeed enhanced, by a national body, that there was an important role for such a body and a real need for proper links to be forged between such a national agency, the regional agencies of local education authorities and the schools themselves. The Trenaman Report reflected this awareness, for example, by recommending that 'the Council should act as a clearing house for information on curricular developments being carried out by other agencies' (DES, 1981, p. 20).

Finally, the work of the Schools Council taught us much about the nature of educational research and its relationship to curriculum change and development. For, although the council was somewhat modest and reticent about its research role, some of its project directors, such as Lawrence Stenhouse and John Elliott, became major figures in the educational research community. They began of course with very practical tasks, but in setting about those tasks they inevitably became involved in research and began to offer many insights into the nature of educational research, whether, for example, it had much in common with scientific research. This in turn involved looking to other disciplines for comparisons and for a suitable model for educational research, especially into the school curriculum. This is a development which was paralleled by similar work in other countries, and especially in the USA, perhaps most notably that of Eliot Eisner, who has been arguing for some time that educational research is, or should be, more human than technical in character (Eisner, 1985). This, then, is a further issue and debate which emerged from the council's work.

It might be argued, therefore, that the main contribution of the council to curriculum development is not to be found in the changes it effected in the curriculum of individual schools. These, as its own Impact and Take-Up Project (Schools Council, 1978) indicated, were relatively small. Rather its importance is to be found in the advances it led to in our understanding of the school curriculum, the issues it raised and required us to address, the insights it offered into the complexities of curriculum planning and development, and the contributions it made to what throughout its lifetime became an ever-accelerating debate, a debate which has largely been brought to a halt by current policies and practice. Its success, then, is to be judged not by the curriculum change it actually brought about but by the quality of the debate it promoted, the way in which it enhanced our thinking about the curriculum and by the research evidence it produced to support that debate and to illuminate that thinking. For it offered us not only theoretical ideas and insights but also empirical evidence of what was actually occurring in schools – very important, if not universally popular, at a time when some people were making wild, unsubstantiated accusations about falling standards and general malpractices. In other words, it faced up to the realities of professional practice and made these the starting point for developing and changing the curriculum.

However, while it was thus contributing massively to debates of this kind within the profession, there was continuous external debate going on about the wisdom of leaving curriculum development and pupil assessment in the hands of a body which was substantially in the control of the teaching profession. The creation of the Schools Council had not been a real victory for the profession but only a skirmish in which it had temporarily gained the upper hand. Politically, people were not happy that teachers should be in control of such an important curriculum development agency, and certainly not happy that teachers should be in control of a body that sponsored examinations and assessment. Parallel with the internal debates within the profession which we have described, therefore, there went on, from a very early stage, a debate in the political arena (Becher and Maclure, 1978).

The prime question being asked in that debate was who should control the school curriculum; and this was a question which emerged through the educational press and in relation to the campaigns which were mounted for parental power in education. This debate, however, was quickly taken up – indeed taken over – by the politicians once they detected this change in public attitude. The issue of teacher control, then, was a burning issue from a very early stage in the life of the Schools Council; and, while it tended first to be explored in the context of parent power, it was increasingly adopted by the politicians.

As the economic climate worsened, a second issue arose, centred on the costs of this kind of curriculum development activity. In reality, the amount of money spent by the Schools Council throughout its life, as we saw earlier, was only a fraction of that spent on research by the DES during the same period. Indeed, there never has been an enormous investment in educational research in the United Kingdom, certainly in comparison to other areas of social interest and activity. Nevertheless, people did begin to say of the Schools Council that a lot of money was being spent and nothing was happening in schools as a result of it. This view was of course strengthened when the council shot itself in the foot by providing evidence of how little was happening in schools as a result of its work in the form of its own Impact and Take-Up Project (Schools Council, 1978). For that project revealed a vast ignorance in schools both of individual projects and of the general work of the council. However, as we suggested earlier, the response to that evidence was somewhat simplistic, since what was of value that emerged from the council's work was evidence of the complexities of the curriculum, the subtleties of curriculum change and development, the centrality of the child and the teacher to this process of change and development and the consequent need for time in which such development, along with a culture of curriculum development, could take root. What the Schools Council's work was telling us was that the curriculum cannot be changed – at least not for the better – in naive ways, that that was why its work was not having much direct impact, but that there are ways in which effective change and development can be supported and promoted.

Both these factors – the political concern about teacher control of curriculum and examinations, and a worsening economic climate – were at the forefront of the considerations which led, first, to a reconstitution of the council, with reduced involvement of teachers at the top management level, and ultimately, in 1984, to the withdrawal of its funding and thus, inevitably, to its demise. Both factors had already come into play in the establishment of other bodies, and especially the Assessment of Performance Unit (APU), whose task was not to change the curriculum but to monitor pupils' performance within it. As we suggested earlier, however, it is difficult to envisage this kind of national monitoring exercise as being implemented with no impact on the curriculum at all. Indeed, as we shall see, this came to be recognized by the APU, which, particularly after the Schools Council had disappeared, accepted a role in curriculum development and became in the latter part of the 1980s, albeit within a somewhat limited compass, the only public source of worthwhile research and publications on curriculum matters. The other sources, such as DES and HMI, saw it as their task to implement government policies by discouraging wider debate and attempting to establish that restricted form of discourse we referred to earlier.

We will consider the work of the APU, along with that of other agencies for the assessment of pupils, shortly. First, however, we must look briefly at the work of an unlikely agency for curriculum change: the Manpower Services Commission (MSC).

## The Manpower Services Commission (MSC)

Perhaps the most effective national agency that we have seen in the United Kingdom was the Manpower Services Commission (MSC). Its arrival on the educational scene in 1982 as a funding agency for schools was greeted with much suspicion and hostility. For there were many people who were concerned about the political significance, and even the impropriety, of funding schools via a branch of the Department of Trade and Industry rather than through the Department of Education and Science and the local education authorities. And there were those too who were disturbed at the strong vocational bias which this agency and this funding route was felt likely to introduce into the secondary school curriculum. Indeed, some local authorities, most notably the Inner London Education Authority (ILEA), refused for a long time to permit their schools to become involved in these initiatives.

Our concern here, however, is not so much with the nature of the curriculum change which this agency brought about as with the effectiveness of the mechanisms by which it sought to effect change. Those mechanisms do not seem to fit readily into any of the categories or match any of the perspectives we explored in Chapter 2. For they were overtly financial and, indeed, commercial. Schools and local authorities were offered large financial inducements to enter into contractual relationships with the MSC for the introduction of courses into their curricula, and/or the making of adjustments to courses already on offer, of a kind which would reflect the goals that the MSC was seeking to attain. Courses which met the criteria established were eligible for quite generous grants in support of their development – grants for equipment, for staffing, for materials and for other resources. At a time of increasing reductions in the levels of resourcing being made available to schools and other educational institutions through the normal funding routes, such inducements were difficult to resist.

Consequently, initiatives such as the Technical and Vocational Educational Initiative (TVEI) established themselves and extended their sphere of influence much more rapidly and widely than any other form of curriculum development has been able to do. They became part and parcel of the secondary school curriculum in a very short time. Furthermore, they did so in spite of the fact that many teachers and others continued to express those reservations about the implications of this kind of development for the nature of educational provision which we mentioned earlier. One can only conclude that if one wants to change the curriculum, then the most effective device one can employ is not to be found in research, in development, in the offering to teachers of interesting and powerful materials, in attempts to persuade them of the value of the changes one is seeking to make, but in the skilful use of bribery, in the offering of levels of resourcing unattainable by other means, in improving significantly the material context in which teachers and pupils work together. In short, the mechanism of change adopted by the MSC was to offer schools contractual relationships through which, in return for, and in support of, the implementation of certain kinds of curriculum change, they were to receive agreed levels of additional funding, a system which has been described in the USA as 'mutual adaption'.

One might of course ask how many teachers 'took the money and ran'. Certainly many of them went to some lengths to justify their 'selling out' to the MSC in such terms. And, indeed, it is quite clear that in many cases the money was taken and used for purposes few would be inclined to quarrel with. Further, it must be recognized that this was invariably done with the full support and approval of the MSC itself, or at least of those who were employed to handle its affairs and distribute its funds.

Nevertheless, again in the context of the central concerns of this book, it must be noted that significant curriculum change was brought about by the MSC, especially through TVEI, and we must emphasize the mechanism and strategy by which this was done, namely the offering to schools of contractual relationships involving significant financial inducements.

A second device employed by those seeking to change the school curriculum by establishing innovations of this kind was the use of the award of accreditation to pupils who successfully completed these new courses and the provision of access to related training schemes through such things as the Youth Opportunities Scheme (YOPS) and the Youth Training Scheme (YTS). This takes us on naturally to our next major section in this discussion of the impact of national agencies on the school curriculum – the influence of agencies for assessment and monitoring.

# THE IMPACT OF AGENCIES FOR ASSESSMENT AND MONITORING

We noted at the beginning of this chapter that curriculum change has sometimes been a by-product of the activities of agencies whose role has been not directly to promote curriculum change as such but to fulfil some other purpose, and which, in attempting to fulfil that purpose have, perhaps inevitably, influenced the curriculum and prompted change within it. For the most part, these have been agencies whose prime concern has been either with monitoring and evaluating the effectiveness of the school system or with assessing the capabilities and achievements of individual pupils. The most notable example of the former is the Assessment of Performance Unit (APU) and of the latter the several examinations boards which have offered certification of various kinds and at various levels to pupils, usually as they are coming to the end of the period of compulsory schooling.

We will look at each of these major influences in turn.

## The Assessment of Performance Unit (APU)

The APU was set up in 1975, in the wake of all the criticisms of schools and accusations of falling standards which had begun to be made in the late 1960s and early 1970s, as a response to those changes which had been occurring both in the curriculum and in the organization of schooling. The APU was established officially in 1975, although plans to set up the unit have been traced to 1970 (Gipps, 1984). Its introduction was low-key and the manner of its establishment was described by one observer as 'shuffling the APU onto the stage in carpet slippers' (Holt, 1981, p. 58). The first public statements about its existence came in the 1974 White Paper on Race Relations, which outlined the government's intention to monitor children's performance in schools in order to identify those with special needs. This intention to monitor performance in order to identify underachievers was repeated in the following year as a result of the recommendations of the Bullock Report on language (DES, 1975). Once established, however, the particular issue of screening to identify special needs was set aside, and the central focus of the APU became the monitoring of standards of performance of pupils in general.

Its terms of reference required it 'to promote the development of methods of assessing and monitoring the achievement of children at school, and to seek to identify the incidence of underachievement'. One of the civil servants who served for a time as administrative head of the unit, Jean Dawson, described its role as follows (Dawson, 1984, p. 125):

> The APU's main purpose is monitoring children's performance, to provide objective information about national standards of children's performance, so that those concerned – teachers, local authorities and central government – may have a reliable and dispassionate measure of the performance of the education system and can then better decide on improvements.

The unit's task, then, was not to change the curriculum, but to discover and to describe, even to 'measure', the performance of the education system.

There is little point, of course, in seeking to obtain this kind of information unless it is planned that something should be done about it. The unit, however, did not see it as its role to change the curriculum, although it did recognize that, if its findings were felt to be of any significance, others would wish to change the curriculum in the light of those findings. Dawson continues:

> We are not a covert agency for curriculum development. Any influence the Unit's work may have on curriculum thinking will be a spin-off from its work on assessment and will happen only if the teachers in the classroom see value in some of the messages emerging from survey findings and wish to use the outcomes of the work in this way.
>
> (ibid.)

This recognition of the significance for the curriculum of the findings of its exercises in monitoring pupil performance was, however, a later development, as we shall see. When it was first established in 1975 it was greeted with some suspicion by the teaching profession for several reasons. First, this was because it was set up with little publicity and almost an aura of secrecy. Second, it was offered as a response to those growing criticisms of schools and accusations of falling standards which we mentioned earlier – the outcries of the Black Papers (Cox and Dyson, 1969a, 1969b; Cox and Boyson, 1977) against the changes which were occurring both in the structure of the school system and in the school curriculum, the general – and unsubstantiated – claims that these changes represented a lowering of educational standards, and especially the events at William Tyndale School and at Risinghill School which, although isolated incidents, were seized upon by those who wished to complain about supposedly falling standards as evidence of their justification in doing so. This view of the purpose and function of the APU was reinforced by the statements of people such as Rhodes Boyson that this kind of national monitoring system was needed in order to provide evidence for the firing of incompetent heads and teachers (Mack, 1976). This in turn implied a deficit view of the school system and a desire to identify and act upon those deficiencies once they had been located (Holt, 1987). Third, it has been argued (Lawton, 1980) that its establishment was a culmination of all the pressure and intrigue which had been going on since the government failed to establish its Curriculum Study Group in the early 1960s and was forced to accept a teacher-controlled Schools Council. And so its advent was seen – rightly as things have turned out – as one of the first steps towards increased political intervention and control in the education system, and ultimately the school curriculum, as 'one step towards the re-establishment of central control' (Kelly, 1977, p. 141). For the existence of deficiencies is a major premise of centralist control, so that charges of deficiency, whether justified or not, are the main excuses for the imposition of central control. In short, it was seen as a body more concerned with discipline and control than with either educational advance or the supporting of curriculum change or development.

However, its subsequent record has done little to substantiate, and much to dispel, the suspicions and concerns with which it was greeted. Its existence must of course be seen as one move in the development of that centralized control which has reached its peak in the National Curriculum and especially its assessment programme. And its status as essentially a *political* agency, financed and thus controlled and directed by the Secretary of State, must also be recognized. For this has meant that it has only been able to mount monitoring exercises in those areas of the curriculum for which the government was prepared to provide the funding, and it has thus been an agency through which the government could make its priorities known, and to some degree felt. In its own conduct of the monitoring exercises, however, it has done much to allay those early fears of its impact and, during the last years of its existence, a good deal to support teachers in certain, albeit somewhat limited, dimensions of curriculum change and development.

Since its establishment in 1975 it has conducted surveys of pupil performance in mathematics (at ages 11 and 15), in English (language) (at ages 11 and 15), in science (at ages 11, 13 and 15), in French, German and Spanish (at age 13) and in Design and Technology (at age 15). It will be seen from that list that its attentions have been directed by its political masters and mistresses towards in the main those areas of the curriculum which were later to become the 'core' subjects of the National Curriculum, so that it has been thus used to declare the government's priorities. Conversely, there may be significance in the areas of the curriculum which were explored but which it was decided should not be monitored – personal and social development, physical development and aesthetic education – since again this may indicate government priorities. Such influence on the curriculum, then, as it has exercised through the choices of subjects to be monitored made for it by its political controllers have been of a kind to stress a view of the curriculum as subject based, an emphasis on certain subjects which seem to have in common more than anything else their economic, instrumental or utilitarian advantages, and a corresponding lack of emphasis on humanities subjects and on education as aesthetic, personal and/or physical development. These influences are of course the responsibility of those who have held the purse-strings and decided on the areas of the curriculum which in their view were the most important and deserved to be made the focus of attention in this way.

Those who have been responsible for implementing these policies, on the other hand, have done so in a far more liberal way and in a manner which has been increasingly supportive of curriculum change and development in the areas they have been asked to address.

First, it should be noted how careful they have been to ensure total anonymity in all the surveys which have been conducted. Far from identifying individual local authorities, schools, headteachers, teachers or even pupils, as demonstrating incompetence (or even competence), every survey has been conducted as a genuinely random exercise in sampling, with no names and thus no pack-drill. So the fears of some, and the hopes of others, that these surveys would produce evidence upon which incompetent heads or teachers might be fired, have been cut short. Furthermore, there has been an emphasis on light sampling, on random sampling and on the voluntary nature of each exercise, schools being free to refuse to accept invitations to participate. And, wherever a battery of tests has been used, no one pupil has been expected to take all of the tests. The emphasis, then, has been on the attempt to obtain a national picture of levels of achievement and attainment, and expressly not to assess the performance of individual schools, teachers or pupils.

There are of course criticisms which can be made of this kind of attempt to *measure* performance and doubts which can be expressed about the accuracy – and thus the value – of evidence obtained in this way. This is not the place, however, to pursue issues of that kind. The concern here is with the impact of these exercises on curriculum change.

Increasingly, attempts have been made to feed back the evidence of these surveys into the system, to make the findings available to teachers in order to support them in their thinking about their own practice and to encourage them in any consequent changes they might wish to make, to support those changes which 'will happen only if the teachers in the classroom see value in some of the messages emerging from survey findings and wish to use the outcomes of the work in that way' (Dawson, 1984, p. 126), as we saw above. In short, it became clear that, once teachers' anxiety was allayed, and they were assured that APU monitoring would not identify weaknesses in particular pupils, teachers, schools or local authorities, the unit was faced with the identical problems of dissemination of ideas from a central source that had been experienced a decade or more earlier by the project teams of the Schools Council. There was almost a sense that unit members were reinventing the wheel in their attempts to disseminate their findings to teachers in schools.

Thus a new publications policy began to emerge in the mid-1980s which involved the production of short reports, on particular aspects of the findings, which were intended to be more accessible to teachers. Several of the monitoring teams were given extended 'lives' to develop new forms of pedagogy deriving from the survey findings. This was the rationale for the establishment of the Children's Learning in Science (CLIS) centre under the direction of Ros Driver at Leeds University, and the Design and Technology team was also given a short extension to produce booklets and other materials for teachers. Thirdly, the more sophisticated test instruments which have been devised in connection with some of the later monitoring exercises, especially those designed to assess the processes of children's learning rather than merely its content, have also been made available for teachers as an aid to their own assessments of their pupils' work (SEAC/EMU, 1991a).

Thus there has emerged a deliberate policy of feeding back into the system by every means available that information produced by the surveys which it was felt might be of help and guidance to teachers in raising the levels of their own performance and in promoting the learning of their pupils. And so the unit, although recognizing its prime role as being to monitor levels of achievement in schools, has come to acknowledge that it can, and should, go beyond that to an attempt to use that evidence and information as a basis for helping teachers to raise their levels of achievement and to change their practices.

It is thus a good example of a body set up to do one thing but, in the process of fulfilling that task, not only having an influence on curriculum development but even coming to recognize that influence and attempting to support and extend it. It is an equally good example, however, of the fact that any such body must work from a restricted and restricting concept of curriculum: that implicit in its original and prime function and/or imposed by its political controllers and those who hold its purse-strings. For the influence it has had – and perhaps the only influence it could have – on curriculum change and development has been largely confined to methods of 'delivery'. That influence has only latterly, through the work of the Design and Technology team, for example, extended to questions about the way in which the curriculum itself is conceived.

The changes towards which its work and its deliberate policy of dissemination have been directed are, largely, changes only in pedagogy, in methodology and approach. The concern has been to find out not merely where children are going wrong but also when, and especially why, so that teachers may adapt their methods and approaches to take account of this. And, while that is of course very valuable, the unit has been permitted to give little attention to the wider and deeper issues which must be addressed if curriculum change and development are to proceed in a properly considered and closely analysed way.

For the unit has had to work from certain predetermined assumptions about the curriculum: that it is a device for transmitting bodies of knowledge, that those bodies of knowledge are encapsulated in certain subjects, that those subjects and their content are to be conceived of in a certain, largely fixed way, that the focus of assessment must be on the testing of the degree to which pupils have assimilated that knowledge, and so on. These assumptions have provided the parameters in which the unit has had to work. They have not in themselves always been recognized as problematic, as themselves being necessary objects of research and monitoring, so that the influence of the unit's work on the school curriculum has been largely confined to improved methods of 'delivery' and has not embraced a questioning of the way in which either the curriculum itself or individual subjects within it are being conceived. There are messages of relevance to that kind of question within the data its surveys have produced, but, for whatever reason – whether political expediency or lack of awareness – those messages have not always been received or disseminated.

In the latter part of its life, particularly after the demise of the Schools Council, the APU did begin to adopt a broader role as an agency for curriculum development and did begin to address some of the wider issues. The Design and Technology exercise, for example, began with a clear statement of the concept of Design and Technology upon which its work was to be based (DES/APU, 1987). And that statement had some influence on the way in which the subject was viewed and conceived in schools as well as on the methods by which it was taught.

Unfortunately, before that dimension of its work could be developed to any significant level, the unit was absorbed into the Educational Monitoring Unit (EMU) of the School Examinations and Assessment Council (SEAC), and became part of the National Curriculum assessment exercise, in which assessment is planned and conducted independently of curriculum development.

There are also lessons to be learnt from several of the surveys about techniques of pupil assessment and, especially, about the merits of particular forms of assessment over others. Much has been learnt, for example, about how we might set about assessing pupil capability in terms of intellectual processes, and educational attainment in terms of the development of those processes, rather than 'measuring' the acquisition and retention of knowledge-content. And the Design and Technology survey offers rich evidence of the advantages of holistic assessment, the assessment of a pupil's overall capability as a step towards the diagnostic analysis of his/her performance, as opposed to the assessment of particular aspects of performance and the aggregation of these into some, perhaps largely meaningless, totality – the approach of the National Curriculum assessment programme. However, such findings take us beyond the political brief of the APU, beyond the wishes of its political controllers, and into areas where much that we are expected to take for granted, and which too often is taken for granted, has to be recognized as being highly problematic. These therefore are findings which are unlikely to be pursued or disseminated widely; indeed, there is every political advantage in suppressing them.

Thus, no matter how valuable its work in relation to teachers' competence as 'deliverers' of a content-based curriculum, the APU has been able to offer little more to curriculum research and development and, unlike the work of the Schools Council, it has not extended our understanding of the complexities of curriculum planning and development. It has certainly not shed light on those logically prior issues of how the curriculum is to be, or may be, conceived, of whether the concept of a particular subject with which we happen to be working at any given time is unchallengeably the only concept which can be adopted or whether our concepts of subjects should not be permitted, indeed encouraged, to change. Nor has it offered insights into whether curriculum change should embrace major reconceptualizations both of curriculum and of its component subjects as well as methods of transmission or 'delivery', and whether effort should be put into discovering ways of assessing these, more complex and more sophisticated, forms of education and of curriculum.

These latter questions, which we saw were raised and faced by bodies such as the Schools Council, the APU, because of its brief and its political base, has been unable for most of its life either to address or even to recognize. Its ultimate impact on the development of the school curriculum, therefore, has been that of contributing to that process, finalized in the National Curriculum, by which our concept of the curriculum has become ossified, and our views of individual subjects have been fixed by their encapsulation in standing orders relating to attainment targets, levels of attainment, programmes of study and all the other paraphernalia of the National Curriculum and its assessment programme.

Thus the work of the APU has now been subsumed under the EMU of the newly created SEAC, where it is not permitted a role in curriculum development of any kind, because that is the responsibility not of the SEAC but of its parallel quango the NCC, and, in any case, there is now no political will to draw lessons for the curriculum which may be seen as a challenge to what has been established as the new status quo.

The APU can be seen in retrospect only as a step towards the creation of national bodies whose task it is not to influence the curriculum nor to support its continuing change and development but to implement government policies and, indeed, to ensure that no change occurs except that which has political sanction.

We will consider the implications of the creation of these bodies in our next major section. First, however, we should give some brief attention to that other main source of indirect influence on the curriculum, the work of national examination boards.

## The influence of the examination boards on the curriculum

It was asserted as long ago as 1868 in the Taunton Report that public examinations must have a restricting influence on the school curriculum. That view was reaffirmed in the Beloe Report (SSEC) in 1960. It is also a view that has entered the folklore of educational mythology, that which substitutes for theory in the minds and the practices of many teachers and others. For many teachers, certainly in the upper reaches of the secondary school, the need to prepare pupils for public examinations has led them almost to opt out of any responsibility for curriculum change or development, the examination syllabuses providing them with a fixed curriculum; and this is often 'an influence which extends to age-ranges well below the fourth and fifth secondary years' (Pudwell, 1983, p. 4). The 11+ selection procedures for secondary transfer are also notorious for their negative effect on the curriculum of the primary school, again not only in its final year.

In more recent times, however, many have come to recognize that, while public forms of examination and assessment must clearly influence and have an impact on the curriculum, that influence and that impact need not be negative, restricting, inhibiting, but that examinations can be framed and new, sophisticated techniques used, in such a way as to influence the curriculum in very positive ways. There are at least two aspects of this.

First, an increasing number of examinations have been planned in such a way as not only to permit but also to invite a degree of freedom of choice for both teacher and pupils. The advent of the 'Mode 3' forms of assessment in the (now defunct) Certificate of Secondary Education (CSE) examinations, that mode which permitted the operation of school-based forms of examining, is one example of a device which sought not to limit freedom beyond what was essential. And the increased use of extended projects in certain subject areas, whether these be practical artefacts in Design and Technology studies, or the written reports and other forms of coursework submitted for assessment in other areas of the curriculum, has also had the effect of reducing the negative impact of examinations and permitting a much greater range and freedom of choice to teachers and pupils. There has also come to be a greater involvement of teachers in the assessment of their own pupils, and this too has not merely minimized the negative impact of public examinations but has also capitalized on the potentially productive links between assessment and curriculum.

Second, however, there have been numerous examples of examinations being used not merely to permit more freedom of action but positively to influence and initiate changes in the curriculum, especially by attempting to bring about changes in the ways in which particular subjects are conceived. There is no doubt, for example, that the manipulation of public examinations played a major role in the conversion of 'handicraft' to 'Craft, Design and Technology' (CDT) (Hicks, 1976), nor that, in the same field, the forms of testing devised for the APU monitoring exercise in this area are currently playing their part in a further reconceptualization of that area of the curriculum. Indeed, it was very largely by this route that the work of the two major Schools Council projects in this area had their impact. In the same way, the council's Geography for the Young School-Leaver project (GYSL), by infiltrating the examination process, influenced the changes which have come about in approaches to geography. There are numerous other examples from almost every area of the curriculum of changes which have been brought about in this way, especially with the aid of those newer and freer examination techniques we have just referred to, as the most casual glance at developments within the new General Certificate of Secondary Education (GCSE) syllabuses will immediately reveal. We noted earlier the imaginative approach the Schools Council adopted towards examinations, and that contributed much to this kind of development.

Furthermore, this reconceptualization has involved rather more than tinkering with subject-matter or knowledge-content. It has in particular been characterized by a focusing on the processes of children's learning. Attempts have been made not only to devise forms of assessment which can reach those processes, as, for example, some of the later test instruments generated by the APU have done, but, further, to do this in order to bring about a change of focus in the curriculum, to encourage teachers to see their work, and even their teaching subjects, in terms not of content to be transmitted and regurgitated, but of processes of intellectual development to be promoted, a view which, as we saw in Chapter 1, represents a first step towards the adoption within education of that 'post-modern' paradigm we discussed there.

There is an inevitable and essential link between assessment and curriculum in all good educational practice. Hitherto, public examinations have been seen as external to this process. Increasingly, however, they have been brought into the equation and attempts have been made to integrate assessment, even that of an external kind, through greater teacher involvement in the process in either the setting or the marking of assessment tasks or sometimes both. In this way, not only has the quality of the assessment process been raised (and almost certainly its accuracy and reliability too), but also – and more centrally to our purposes here – the role of assessment in curriculum change has been enhanced.

Public examinations and assessment have come to be recognized, then, as very powerful tools for bringing about curriculum change. Increasingly they have come to be used in this way. They are still, however, equally powerful tools for inhibiting change and for exercising external control over the school curriculum. It is clearly in this light that they are viewed in the context of the National Curriculum assessment programme, whose prime concern is, first, to establish this new curriculum and, second, to maintain it in much its present form, to achieve centralized control of the curriculum and, especially, of curriculum change. The National Curriculum and its assessment programme are to be implemented through the agency of three newly created national bodies: the National Curriculum Council (NCC), the Curriculum Council for Wales (CCW) and the School Examinations and Assessment Council (SEAC). It is to an evaluation of their implications for curriculum change that we now turn.

## AGENCIES FOR POLICY IMPLEMENTATION AND CONTROL

It is not possible to say very much about the three bodies which have been created to implement the new National Curriculum policies. They have not existed long enough to have achieved anything of note. In any case our interest in them in the context of this book must focus on the role they have in relation to curriculum change along with their likely influence on it.

We should note first that they mark a very deliberate separating of curriculum from assessment, so that, if we were right to claim that the two are integral to each other and that a judicious combination of the two is a major aid to curriculum change, we can perhaps deduce that their separation in the new order indicates an intention that there be little or no curriculum change, and certainly none that is brought about by those within the schools.

The role of NCC and CCW is to draw up the details of the school curriculum within the listing of subjects and the other curricular requirements of the 1988 Education Reform Act. They do this, however, only to advise the Secretary of State, who then translates their recommendations, if he or she is so minded, into statutory orders. These orders then become the school curriculum in the sense that they lay down what is to be taught in all state-maintained schools. Change, therefore, can only be effected by having those orders altered, and thus only by the Secretary of State; and that would be a very long, tortuous and difficult process. It is also a political rather than an educational process. Scope exists for teachers to modify and adjust their methods, the techniques by which they 'deliver' this curriculum package. Such scope, however, has little significance when the curriculum itself is determined politically and can only be changed through the appropriate political procedures.

It is obvious, therefore, that the officers of NCC and CCW embark upon their task of introducing the National Curriculum to schools from a position of unprecedented power in comparison with the other central agencies we have considered. The change strategy is, in terms of the perspectives we considered in Chapter 2, power-coercive. It cannot be assumed, however, that power to make teachers act in particular ways is necessarily the most effective strategy for improving the quality of the curriculum or for raising standards in schools. For, as Helen Simons (1988, p. 85) argues, 'Anyone with enough power can change schools for the worse. How to change them for the better is the problem'. She goes on to remind us that evidence shows that the power-coercive and centralized strategies which were adopted in the USA during a period of twenty years from 1965 have had the effect of lowering standards of pupil performance in American schools rather than raising them.

Furthermore, the dissemination strategy which has been adopted is essentially of a centre–periphery kind, using a 'cascade' methodology.

Indeed, one might even call it a 'deluge' methodology, since the process so far has been one of saturating schools and other institutions, such as those concerned with teacher training, with floods of documentation which purports to tell teachers how to carry out what the law now requires of them. The process is a simple one of demanding change by the power-coercive strategy of the law and attempting to ensure it is implemented by offering teachers written advice and/or instruction – a device whose ineffectiveness is more than familiar to anyone who has spent any time at all engaged in the complexities of teacher education or re-education.

The National Curriculum for England and Wales is not a curriculum which acknowledges the need for constant or continuous evaluation and change. Rather its concern is to arrest change, once it has established itself as the new school curriculum. It is not a curriculum which recognizes the value of those changes we referred to earlier which have transformed our conceptions of almost every curriculum subject or area. Rather its concern is to take them back to where they started, or, if this is not the *intention*, it is likely to be the *effect* in many areas of the curriculum. And it is not a curriculum which emphasizes the processes of children's learning. Rather it stresses the content of that learning and the 'aims and objectives' of teaching. It thus reflects on many fronts that Newtonian paradigm we noted in Chapter 1, which sees all as fixed and stable and as a status quo to be preserved, and which sees learning and the curriculum as cumulative rather than as transformative (Doll, 1989). Thus, if current policies are built on any notion of change at all, it is a Newtonian rather than an Einsteinian concept, but, worse, it is a concept not of change as being for the better but as very much for the worse, since that can be the only reason for seeking to halt it.

The role of SEAC in this exercise is to reinforce the process of bringing about and maintaining the desired changes by developing a system of external assessment and examinations at four 'key-stages', 7+, 11+, 14+ and 16+, which by testing the extent to which pupils have assimilated the content of this curriculum will ensure that what they are offered is what the law requires. Its role is, therefore, to assist in the process of inhibiting subsequent change.

The teams it has commissioned to develop these standard assessment tasks (SATs) are attempting to build on those insights into the assessment process and its links with curriculum which we noted earlier. There are limits to what they can do, however, within the confines of the predetermined curriculum those SATs are supposed to assess, and, indeed, within the close control of their steering committees. And in any case it has now been made clear by the Secretary of State that, at least at key-stage 3 (14+), 'the process will be more manageable and the results will command more confidence if the tests are mainly in the form of short written tests' (press release 22/91, 25 January 1991). Whether such tests will tell us anything worth knowing is a matter for debate, despite the Secretary of State's confident assertion that they 'will provide a fair and objective measure of pupils' abilities' (ibid.) and that 'they will command public confidence' (ibid.). What concerns us here, however, is that their impact on the curriculum will be a negative rather than a positive one, so that they too will assist in the process of arresting and inhibiting curriculum change.

These tests, then, must also be seen as part of that power-coercive strategy by which the changes required by the 1988 Education Reform Act and the compulsory National Curriculum it created are imposed upon schools. The form that the tests are now taking reveals very clearly that, in spite of the rhetoric of raising standards, their prime purpose is to support the process of establishing and maintaining the new curriculum.

We must note, however, one interesting feature which appears to be emerging from the activity of SAT development. Where the SATs are non-statutory, as, for example, is the case with those designed to test Design and Technology at key-stage 1 (7+), where teachers do not have to accept them or use them if they do not find them worthwhile or supportive of their classroom activities, where they cannot be imposed by law so that power-coercive strategies cannot be used, every effort is being made to produce not merely appropriate forms of test but also corresponding teaching materials of a kind to which teachers will respond positively. The law requires that Design and Technology be included in the curriculum of first and infant schools, but, since the testing of it is non-statutory, teachers will only accept what is offered by the SAT development teams if it is seen to provide them with a means of introducing this kind of work into the curriculum in a manner they regard as satisfactory and even productive. In this context, therefore, the strategy has to be empirical–rational or normative–re-educative, albeit within a framework of compulsory requirements. As such, it appears, even at this early stage, that it is achieving some success. This is an area in which teachers need help; and it is one in which they can be offered that help through the provision of valuable materials and through in-service support. The process is also one in which there is more reason to hope that change of an effective kind will be brought about than in those areas where the strategies are essentially power-coercive, and where the compulsory tests in themselves are being used as a device to assure implementation and compliance.

One of the strengths of empirical–rational and normative–re-educative approaches is that they genuinely seek to involve teachers themselves in the process of change. Without this, it is unlikely that change can be effective in any real sense. What is also worth noting, however, is that, when one does not involve teachers at all stages of the change process, not only does this reduce its efficiency, it does so in part because it has the effect of lowering teacher morale and undermining teacher confidence. The current policy of creating and establishing a National Curriculum for England and Wales is predicated on a deficit view of the teaching profession. The implementation of that policy is conceived, planned and carried out by instruction and dictation to teachers – much of it from non-professional sources. It cannot be seen as a policy which will raise teachers' views of themselves, either individually or collectively, despite the rhetoric. And it is difficult to understand how anyone can reasonably expect to bring about improvement in a system by a process of downgrading, demoralizing or deskilling its practitioners.

We should note finally that the authors of these policies have learned nothing from the Schools Council's experience which we explored earlier, derived from its attempts to bring about curriculum change from outside the schools, nor from any of those other insights which we saw in Chapter 2 have been developed from many attempts at curriculum change. The subtleties and complexities of *actually* changing the curriculum, whatever view of change one takes, have gone unrecognized and unacknowledged. It must be highly questionable, therefore, whether these procedures will in the event bring about the change that is intended, although there can be little doubt that they will be very effective in ensuring that no further planned change occurs beyond that.

## SUMMARY AND CONCLUSIONS

In this chapter we have looked at the work of a number of national agencies which have set out to influence or change the school curriculum. In doing so, we have identified a number of important issues, both theoretical and practical, which their work has brought to light. It has been shown that, although the form and status of these agencies may be different, and their consequent power to influence teachers may vary, all face the problem of disseminating their ideas to schools. And all highlight in their respective ways, the flaws in centre–periphery or RD&D models of change. When this issue of dissemination is addressed professionally, as in the work of the Schools Council, a new, more sophisticated and subtle role can be identified for national agencies. They can act as clearing houses for important new ideas and can thereby develop the insights of the profession at every level. They can become providers of materials to challenge reflective practitioners. They can provide the focal point for the professional debate which is so essential to developments in professional practice. When the issue of dissemination is not addressed, however, the central agency's work will either be ignored, or it will be altered beyond recognition, or it will serve to undermine the confidence of teachers, according to the power and perceived status of the change agent.

Perhaps the most crucial issue that has been highlighted in this chapter is that the success of any central agency in changing the school curriculum hinges on the relationships that it is able to form with, and the status that it affords to, the individual teacher in school.

It is for this reason that recent years have seen the focus of attention shift from national agencies to the teacher as the major change agent in relation to the school curriculum, as it has come to be recognized increasingly that, to be effective, change must occur at the deepest levels of professional practice. It is thus to an exploration of school-centred innovation that we turn in Chapter 4.

# 4

# SCHOOL-CENTRED INNOVATION

In the 1970s an alternative approach to curriculum innovation emerged, characterized by a commitment to promoting practitioners, both collectively and individually, as the principal agents of change. The problems of practitioners rather than the ideas of innovators were now seen as the logical starting point in promoting change. It would be misleading, however, to imply that such a view had its genesis in the 1970s. On the contrary, it was enshrined in the constitution of the Schools Council (1973, p. 54) which stated that 'regard shall at all times be had to the general principle that each school should have the fullest possible measure of responsibility for its own work, with its own curriculum and teaching methods based on the needs of its own pupils and evolved by its own staff'. Moreover, many of the Schools Council's projects took as their starting point innovative practices already existing, or in the process of being established, in schools. But during the 1970s the idea of 'grass roots' innovation gained new impetus and, more significantly perhaps, acquired a more fully articulated theoretical base. This shift in the locus of initiative from the centre to the periphery was endorsed by the Schools Council. From the mid-1970s onwards it virtually abandoned the use of research, development and diffusion (RD&D) strategies for promoting change and adopted instead a policy of supporting school-based 'problem-solving' alternatives.

Over the next ten years there emerged a plethora of decentralized practices such as school-based curriculum development, school-focused in-service education of teachers (INSET), school self-evaluation, whole school review and action research. The significant feature of these practices, at least in theory, is the central involvement of practitioners; an involvement, moreover, that is voluntary rather than coerced and that is perceived by participants to address their own individual or institutional needs. Hargreaves (1982) proposes the generic term school-centred innovation to encompass all these practices on the grounds that they are underpinned by a common ideology embodying the principles of participation, collaboration, democracy and diversity. For want of a more appropriate term, school-centred innovation is adopted in this book in the generic sense proposed by Hargreaves, but with one proviso. School-centred innovation should not imply that all curriculum activity and decision-making takes place at the school level. It is conceivable that an outside initiative – an examination syllabus, a centrally disseminated project, a local authority scheme, etc. – could provide the stimulus or catalyst for school-centred innovation. Edwards (1983), for example, describes how the American social studies project *Man: A Course of Study* provided the impetus and the model for a group of humanities teachers to develop and extend their own innovatory practices.

## SCHOOL-CENTRED INNOVATION – THE ORIGINS

The origins of this movement are complex but it is possible to identify a number of interrelated factors which contributed to its increasing popularity in the 1970s.

By the early 1970s the limitations of centre–periphery strategies for promoting change, albeit modified in the work of the Schools Council, were becoming increasingly apparent. As previously indicated, there had already been a substantial shift in the concerns of curriculum innovators, researchers and theorists from the centre to the periphery; from a focus on development and diffusion/dissemination to a focus on adoption, implementation and institutionalization. From this work emerged a view that substantial and lasting change was contingent upon the active involvement of practitioners in the process. For example, Shipman (1973, p. 52), the evaluator of the Keele Integrated Studies Project, recognized that 'the successful organization of planning curriculum change may depend more on mobilizing teachers into planning and implementing than on getting schools to accept packaged materials'. In a similar vein, MacDonald and Rudduck (1971, p. 149), members of the Humanities Curriculum Project team, acknowledged that 'curriculum development will not be effective in the long term unless it is seen to be capable of being tailored to the circumstances and temper of particular schools and individual teachers'. Such views were supported by research evidence which suggested that schools involved with central teams in the development and trialling of ideas and materials were more likely to sustain innovation than schools that became involved during a secondary trialling stage or through the mass dissemination of the final product. The further away from the centre of the activity the less the likelihood of substantial and lasting change.

A number of features characterized the failure of RD&D strategies for promoting change. There was often a mismatch between the values and expectations of the 'superordinate group' responsible for the development and promotion of an innovation and the 'subordinate group' of teachers whose main concern was with its implementation. Differences in the definitions and interpretations of the two groups resulted in widespread 'cannibalization' whereby teachers, at least in the eyes of the developers, violated the integrity of innovations by incorporating chosen elements into their prevailing practices. Alternatively, these differences led to a phenomenon described by MacDonald and Rudduck (op.cit., p. 151) as 'innovation without change'.

A common problem of RD&D was the tendency for teachers to invest innovations with an authority that denied their own independent judgements (MacDonald and Rudduck, op.cit.). Ironically, this was evident even with teachers involved in the Humanities Curriculum Project: a project which specifically set out to encourage teachers to take a research stance towards their own practice. In evaluating the dissemination of this project, Humble and Simon (1978) found that teachers tended to seek judgements from the project team whom they regarded as experts. In its most extreme or, perhaps, cynical form teachers interpreted the role of the project team in terms of 'you're paid to tell us' (Rudduck and Kelly, 1976, p. 86).

A further failure reflected the inability of teachers and pupils to come to terms with the new roles demanded of them. Unfortunately, these difficulties were often 'perceived as incompetencies rather than transitional steps' (Humble and Simon, 1978, p. 165) and were compounded by the inability of schools to provide the organizational framework and leadership necessary to support institutional members through the uncertainties of innovation.

In relation to Britain it has been argued that the devolved nature of the educational system, coupled with the degree of autonomy enjoyed by schools and individual teachers, is not conducive to RD&D strategies of change. As Humble and Simons (op.cit., p. 169) suggest, 'centrally-conceived innovation is somewhat at odds with an

educational system which is locally administered and where autonomy
for curricular decision-making is said to lie with the schools'. In such
circumstances, innovation may have to be negotiated at a number of
levels and with a diverse constituency before it reaches the classroom.
The situation, of course, has changed radically in recent years with the
implementation of the 1988 Education Reform Act. The autonomy of
teachers has been significantly curtailed through the imposition of
a centrally prescribed curriculum, and local authorities have been
marginalized by the devolution of financial management to schools.
Additionally, examining bodies, in some instances in the past instigators of curriculum innovation, have been subjected to greater central
control through, for example, GCSE national criteria and Clause 5
of the 1988 Act which states that 'no course of study leading to a
qualification . . . shall be provided for pupils . . . unless the Secretary
of State or a designated body gives approval' (DES, 1988b). It is
conceivable, therefore, that endeavours in the future to bring about
change on a centre–periphery basis will be more 'successful' in terms
of implementation than those of the past. We raised in the last
chapter, however, the question of how genuine, and in whose interests,
such change is likely to be.

The difficulties encountered in attempting to promote change
through RD&D strategies led to a growing recognition that the school
as an organization played a decisive role in determining the likelihood
of an innovation 'taking root'. Consequently, there was a substantial
shift in emphasis from dissemination and adoption to implementation
and institutionalization as the key focus of attention in the process. In
particular, attempts were made to identify the characteristics of schools
that were conducive to the successful implementation of innovation. For example, Ross (1958, p. 24) used the term 'adaptability' to
indicate 'the capacity of a school to take on new practices and discard
outmoded ones'. For Nisbet (1974, p. 10) the 'creativity' of a school
was 'its capacity to adopt, adapt, generate or reject innovations', and
for Hoyle (1975, p. 329) 'the capacity to sustain innovation'. Miles
(1965) saw schools in terms of 'organizational health', that is 'a school
system's ability not only to function effectively, but to develop and
grow into a more fully functioning system' (cited in Hoyle 1969,
p. 231). Extending Miles's medical metaphor, Hoyle (ibid.) highlighted
the problem of 'tissue rejection' whereby 'innovation does not take
with a school because the social system of the school is unable to
absorb it into its normal functioning'. Collectively, this work is significant on two counts. First, it marked the beginning of a substantial

shift in curriculum innovation from the centre to the periphery by establishing the school as the crucial unit in the change process. Second, its constituent metaphors convey an image of schools as organic systems, capable of continuous growth and self-renewal. This contrasts sharply with the more mechanistic and instrumental image of schools inherent in top-down models of change and in current concerns with performance indicators, school effectiveness and quality control.

The 1960s heralded the onset of a period of unprecedented and rapid social, technological and economic change. In many instances school-centred innovation was undoubtedly a pragmatic response to these changes. Schools were presented with novel situations to which they were forced to respond. The raising of the school leaving age in 1972 confronted schools with the problem of engaging for a further two years a cohort of pupils who, as its losers, rejected emphatically the elitist system of traditional education, together with the watered-down academic curriculum to which many of them were subjected. At the same time many schools were endeavouring to come to terms with the realities of comprehensivization. Some responded by clinging to traditional tripartite divisions and practices. Others, however, embraced the egalitarian principles underpinning comprehensive education and undertook a fundamental reappraisal of their organizational structures and curricular provisions. Rising unemployment in the late 1970s and early 1980s heralded another wave of innovation as schools grappled with the problem of containing increasing numbers of disaffected pupils. Further developments in the curriculum occurred in response to equal opportunities legislation. Collectively, these changes spawned a plethora of new organizational, curricular and pedagogical practices. The extent to which these changes were genuinely innovative, however, is a moot point.

Another explanation for school-centred innovation is essentially financial. The recession and oil crisis of the 1970s created a climate in which questions of value for money assumed increasing significance in political circles. By the mid-1970s the curriculum development movement in Britain was 'in "cold storage", awaiting an economic thaw' (MacDonald and Walker, 1976, p. 2). In these circumstances school-centred innovation offered an attractive alternative to the high-cost centrally developed projects of the Schools Council. Partial melting occurred in the 1980s as substantial financial resources were poured into education, primarily to offset the problem of rising unemployment, but also in a misdirected attempt to reverse Britain's economic fortunes. Ironically, most of this money was channelled through the Manpower Services Commission, a national agency outside the jurisdiction of the Department of Education and Science but one which played a central role in promoting curriculum change during this period, as we saw in Chapter 3.

It would be misleading to explain the growth of school-centred innovation in the 1970s as primarily a reaction to the failure of RD&D or as a response to changing social circumstances. During the 1970s a learner-centred, 'progressive' view of education gained ascendancy, and took root particularly in British primary schools following the Plowden Report (CACE, 1967). Central to 'progressive' ideology is the view that education should start from the experiences and concerns of the learner. It follows from this that teachers should have maximum freedom in curriculum decision-making in order to exploit fully the educational potential of their pupils' experiences and of the unique features of the locality in which they practice. Thus, school-centred innovation is seen as an integral part of this progressivist educational ideology. Allied to this, and partly constitutive of it, was the articulation in the 1970s of a number of conceptions of curriculum and teacher development which again emphasized the centrality of the teacher in curriculum decision-making. Most notable, perhaps, was Stenhouse's research model of curriculum which envisaged teachers as a community of researchers engaged in a continuing process of enquiry into their own educational practices, developing their professional understanding as a consequence. The establishment of the Classroom Action Research Network in Britain could be seen as the practical realization of this educational vision. The pivotal role of teacher development in effecting change is a recurring theme in educational literature. In the early 1960s Taba (1962, p. 447) drew attention to a 'grass roots' approach to curriculum development in the USA based on the assumption that 'the functioning curriculum would be improved only as the professional competence of teachers improved'. A decade later, 'no curriculum development without teacher development' became the rallying cry of the Humanities Curriculum Project team (Stenhouse, 1980, p. 40). For Fullan (1982, p. 108), 'educational change depends on what teachers do and think – it is as simple and as complex as that'. And, lest the message be too easily forgotten, Bliss (1990, p. 143) reminds us that 'in talking about innovation in schools we are talking not about bringing things into the school but about changing the thinking and the practice of people'.

If there is no curriculum development without teacher development the converse is equally true. The relationship between curriculum development and teacher development is essentially dialectical. One does not logically precede the other. It is both within and through curriculum development that significant teacher development takes place. Therefore, to deny teachers opportunities to engage with the problematics of curriculum is to deny them the means of enhancing their professional understanding.

Having outlined the origins of school-centred innovation, we now turn our attention to an examination of some of the forms that it has taken.

## SCHOOL-BASED CURRICULUM DEVELOPMENT

Skilbeck (1984a, p. 2) defines school-based curriculum development as 'the planning, design, implementation and evaluation of a programme of students' learnings by the educational institution of which these students are members'. It could be argued that this is a reasonably apt description of what went on in most British schools prior to the introduction of the National Curriculum and, as such, implies nothing distinctive about school-based curriculum development. However, he elaborates: 'the institution should be a living educational environment defined and defining itself as a distinct entity and characterized by a definite pattern of relationships, aims, values, norms, procedures and roles. The curriculum in school-based curriculum development is internal and organic to the institution not an extrinsic imposition'.

In an earlier paper, Skilbeck (1975) defines more clearly the distinctive characteristics of school-based curriculum development. He views the curriculum as being made up of experiences 'of value, developed by the teacher and learner together from a close and sympathetic appraisal of the learner's needs and his [sic] characteristics as a learner' (p. 18). It follows from this that 'freedom for both teachers and pupils is a necessary condition for the full educational potential of these experiences to be realized' (ibid.). Skilbeck expresses considerable confidence in the professional competency of teachers to engage in school-based curriculum development. He recognizes that curriculum development is 'an intellectually demanding and onerous task' (op.cit., p. 19) but believes that teachers, if suitably trained, have the capacity to carry it out. Success, however, 'depends upon the development of quite substantial support systems' including 'an extensive in-service education programme' (ibid.).

If Skilbeck's definition of school-based curriculum development is accepted it has to be recognized that it implies more than a question of the locus of control in curriculum decision-making, although this is a central issue. It implies a particular educational ideology which goes beyond this question.

Skilbeck goes on to present a model of school-based curriculum development comprising a linear sequence of activities. The sequence commences with 'situational analysis', proceeds through the stages of 'goal formation', 'programme building' and 'interpretation and implementation' and finally culminates in 'monitoring, feedback, assessment, reconstruction'. Needless to say, the final stage is fed back into 'situational analysis' prior to the initiation of a further sequence of development. In his articulation of this model there are a number of tensions and contradictions which need to be highlighted.

It is clear that he unequivocally accepts the logic of the classical Tylerian model of curriculum planning, yet attempts to argue that 'it is not committed to means–ends reasoning'. He states categorically that 'curriculum development at the school level *must* start, *not* (emphasis added) with given objectives or objectives drawn up abstractly, but with a critical appraisal of the situation'. He further emphasizes that 'it is with this situation that the teacher must start his [*sic*] analysis'. He subsequently contradicts this position by advocating that there may be sound institutional or psychological reasons for intervening first at any one of the stages. Indeed, he goes on to claim that the model '*encourages* them (the practitioners) to enter the model at any stage they wish' (emphasis added). Apart from the obvious contradiction, the suggestion that the user may enter at any stage is not consistent with the logic of the objectives model of planning, including the modified version he offers. The objectives model is inherently means–ends in its reasoning. If the various stages constitute, as he claims, 'the elements of the curriculum development process' then they have to proceed in a linear fashion. Situational analysis is carried out in order to clarify goals. It is therefore, by definition, both logically and practically prior. In turn, goal formation is an essential prerequisite to programme building, and so on. The rationale of the model insists that there is no proper basis for programme building until goals have been clarified. Therefore to enter the model at this latter stage, even if the proper sequence is then adhered to, is logical and practical nonsense.

A further important point needs to be made in relation to the model Skilbeck advocates. In our view he is naive in believing that a 'situational analysis' of the diverse and invariably conflicting demands that impinge upon educational practice could lead to a coherent and consensual set of goals. There appears to be an a priori assumption in his model that conflicting values can and should be reconciled as a prerequisite to curriculum development. We take the opposite view that curriculum development is an expression of and response to value conflict; that the curriculum provides the means for an exploration of educational values rather than the means for their reconciliation.

From this analysis it should be evident that it is misleading to assume that technical rationality pertains only to centre–periphery strategies of change. Throughout Skilbeck's work there appears to be a persistent and irreconcilable tension between the technicist, goal-oriented assumptions implicit in the model he endorses and his advocacy of education as experience and of the curriculum development process as an organic whole. And, as will be argued later, this is equally true of a number of other strategies that are used for promoting school-centred innovation.

Hargreaves (1982) draws attention to the rhetoric of school-centred innovation in contrast to the reality. He claims that discussions and commentaries on school-centred innovation have focused on 'the virtues and successes' while the 'drawbacks and failures' (op.cit., p. 252) are virtually unexamined. The literature of school-centred innovation is characterized by a 'dearth of rigorous, critical and empirically grounded accounts of particular schemes and projects' (op.cit., p. 253). Of the accounts that are available, Hargeaves typifies three categories.

Exhortatory accounts issue 'spirited moral and professional injunctions' (ibid.) in an attempt to persuade people of the importance of school-centred innovation and why it should take place. Embodied in these accounts is a form of symbolic discourse – using terms such as 'participation' and 'self-development' – that has very little explanatory power. The accounts are vague, providing little guidance about the forms school-centred innovation might take or the problems that might be encountered.

Taxonomic accounts take for granted the merits of school-centred innovation and through the 'hypothetical and conditional language of the possible' outline in detail the many different kinds that might be developed. Hargreaves cites the work of Henderson and Perry (1981) as an exemplar of this genre.

Reflective accounts report actual instances of school-centred innovation in the form of 'journalistic recollections' (op.cit., p. 257) written by leading participants. Such accounts tend to focus on the apparent successes of innovation. While not questioning the honesty and integrity of the writers, Hargreaves advocates caution in relation to these accounts in that they lack the rigour associated with empirically grounded research.

Hargreaves's typology could be adapted to apply to the literature on educational change in general. In response to any educational initiative, for example the Technical and Vocational Educational Initiative (TVEI), profiling, GCSE, records of achievement, etc., the literature which emerges appears to follow a particular sequence, although, as would be expected, there is some overlap. Initially, accounts are of the kind described by Hargreaves: exhortatory, taxonomic and reflective. Collectively, these accounts are associated with the implementation stage. These are quickly followed by more rigorous empirically grounded accounts, generated in the main by educational researchers. This constitutes the empirical stage. In the final stage, research findings are analysed in relation to wider social and educational meta-theory. This could be seen as the analytical stage.

An examination of the literature of school-centred innovation seems to bear out Hargreaves's claim. The work of Skilbeck examined above could be categorized as part exhortatory, part taxonomic. It has no empirical base. Three significant collections, Eggleston (1980), Skilbeck (1984c) and Bolam (1982), consist largely of anecdotal accounts of school-centred innovation written by practitioners. In some, development constitutes little more than tinkering with the overall structure of the curriculum, particularly in relation to the fourth- and fifth-year option system. Few, if any, focus explicitly on the curriculum in terms of its actual implementation in the classroom. An example taken from Skilbeck's collection serves to illustrate this point. One of the contributors (the head of a school), in a position paper on school-based review which recommended minor adjustments in the overall structure of the curriculum, concludes:

> I am sure that all will appreciate the value of a tough minded look at our curriculum. It is not surprising that a good comprehensive school like Henbury has developed a sound working curriculum. It is a tribute to all who teach and have taught in Henbury that *the refinements required are fairly small.*
>
> (op.cit., p. 108, emphasis added)

Indeed, these collections lend support to the findings of Knight (1985). In a meta-analysis of fifty written accounts, the practice described was so heterogeneous that he is led to question the generic use of the term school-based curriculum development. Although there are methodological shortcomings in his analysis, it still casts doubts on the efficacy of school-based curriculum development to bring about substantive change. In the majority of the accounts examined, development had taken place within the context of traditional subjects. There were few examples of whole school approaches to change, as advocated in the exhortatory accounts of school-based curriculum development. On the evidence of the research, Knight concludes that 'if school-based curriculum development acts to enhance teachers as professionals, then . . . it is more likely to do so by developing them as a teacher of a subject or subjects than it is to develop them as educationalists' (op.cit., p. 44). This of course should not be seen as a criticism of school-based curriculum development *per se* but as a comment on the way it is manifested in practice in many schools.

Other researchers have responded to Hargreaves's challenge by providing rigorous, empirically grounded case studies of school-centred innovation. The most interesting aspect of this research is that it brings to the surface the ideological and micropolitical dimensions of school-initiated change which are invariably downplayed or ignored in exhortatory, taxonomic and reflective accounts. As Sparkes (1987, p. 38) observes, 'it is likely that ideological differences and conflict of interest will be brought into sharp relief when attempts to create change are instigated'. It has already been noted that during the curriculum development movement of the 1960s and early 1970s endeavours to promote change in the curriculum gave rise to the phenomenon of 'innovation without change'. This has proved to be no less true of school-centred innovation. Commitment to the central values of such innovation – participation, ownership, negotiation, etc. – has been exposed in practice to be a form of self-deluding rhetoric. A number of studies highlight the strategies whereby teachers have created an illusion of innovation without any significant change occurring in practice.

The studies of Patriarca and Buchmann (1983), Sparkes (1987) and Kirk (1988) show how school-centred innovation generates its own discursive practice. In each case innovation led to a particular kind of discourse which they categorized as 'tribal rhetoric', 'strategic rhetoric' and 'formal doctrine' respectively. Kirk (op.cit., p. 452) describes how the formal doctrine was created 'as the innovative idea was increasingly articulated in a formal, systematic and integrated way'. It represented an idealization of the innovation but was found to be dysfunctional in relation to actual practice. It acted as a facade and served as a crucial device for communicating the legitimacy of the innovative idea within the wider school organization. Similarly, for

Patriarca and Buchmann (op.cit., p. 416–7), tribal rhetoric 'was a self-supporting phenomenon with ritual functions . . . it became a symbol of change, movement, and innovation . . . words succeeded and made people feel successful; the fate of the policies, however, seemed uncertain'.

Sparkes's (1987) research tells a similar story. It illustrates how a group of physical educators 'developed the strategic use of certain language forms in relation to the proposed innovation, as a means of enhancing the status of their subject within the school' (op.cit., p. 37). Futhermore, it indicates that the use of such rhetoric, 'directed at certain significant publics' (p. 42), necessitates little if any change in classroom practice.

It becomes evident from these studies that school-centred innovations, no less than their centrally directed counterparts, have to negotiate the existing micropolitical, cultural, biographical and socio-historical milieux of schools. Thus, they do not necessarily replace old practices but establish an uneasy co-existence alongside them. In Patriarca and Buchmann's study certain aspects of the traditional curriculum remained sacrosanct, resulting in a phenomenon they termed 'growth by addition' whereby 'new content simply had to be added and fitted into pre-existent curricular and programme categories' (p. 416). Likewise, Kirk's (1988) study demonstrates the persistence in innovations of residual ideologies from previous practices.

These studies serve to highlight a number of other significant features pertaining to school-centred innovation. First, school-centred innovation does not necessarily imply common understanding and shared meaning. On the contrary, participants may adopt different orientations towards the innovation, reflecting their own individual biographies, personal beliefs, values and aspirations. Second, school-centred innovation is not time-bound; it has its own temporality. The innovative idea itself is shaped or even transformed in the process of execution. Third, participation in innovation is not equally distributed. Likewise, decision-making is not equally shared.

Kirk concludes by reiterating the concern expressed by Hargreaves that school-centred innovation could be a cover for 'back-door centralism' through the ideological manipulation of teachers. Events in Britain have of course moved on with the imposition of a national curriculum. This, however, does not negate this concern, for the agencies responsible for its implementation utilize with impunity the legitimating rhetoric of school-centred innovation, as we shall see again in Chapter 5.

# ACTION RESEARCH

Action research as a mode of enquiry is not new and, contrary to general belief, neither is its application to educational contexts a recent phenomenon. Its origins are attributed to the social psychologist Kurt Lewin. Its potential application to educational settings was recognized in the USA in the early 1950s (Corey, 1953), although there is little evidence to suggest it made any substantial impact. Its emergence in Britain during the 1970s has been attributed almost exclusively to the work of Lawrence Stenhouse and his colleagues at the Centre for Applied Research in Education, University of East Anglia (McNiff, 1988). From here it has spread to other sites and now finds expression in a range of educational contexts. Its logic underpins a number of initial teacher education courses and local authority INSET provision. Many universities model their diploma and MA courses around action research activities. The theoretical underpinnings of action research are diverse and advocates have drawn on a range of intellectual traditions to substantiate and justify their work. These include Aristotle's ethics, the moral philosophy of MacIntyre, Gadamer's hermeneutics, the dialectics of Hegel and Marx, and the critical theory of Habermas. It is not our intention to examine the methods by which action research is accomplished but, rather, to assess its educational rationale, validity and potential.

Educational action research is not easy to define, owing partly to wide variations in the interpretations of its purposes, methodologies and theoretical perspectives. By way of illustration, it has been defined as:

> the process by which practitioners attempt to study their problems scientifically in order to guide, correct and evaluate their decisions and actions
>
> (Corey 1953, p. 6)
>
> the study of a social situation with a view to improving the quality of action within it
>
> (Elliott, 1981, p. 1)
>
> concerned with the development and testing of strategies for realizing educational value *in* (author's emphasis) action
>
> (Elliott, 1983, p. 243)
>
> a form of self-reflective inquiry undertaken by participants in educational situations in order to improve the rationality, justice and satisfactoriness of (a) their own social and educational prac-

tices, (b) their understanding of these practices and (c) the institutions and situations in which these practices are carried out

(Kemmis, 1988, p. 156)

inquiry teachers undertake to understand and improve their own practice

(McCutcheon and Jung, 1990, p. 143)

Although they share a number of common assumptions, these definitions serve to highlight some of the tensions in how action research is understood and practised in educational contexts. Some action researchers place emphasis on the generation of empirically grounded knowledge, others on the improvement of practice. Elliott (1991, p. 49), for example, makes his position clear. For him, the fundamental aim of action research is 'to improve practice rather than to produce knowledge'. The latter he sees as 'subordinate to, and conditioned by' (ibid.), the former. Another group cast action research as a radical, emancipatory project of freeing individuals from the ideological and material structures which impinge upon and constrain their practices. In effect these different interpretations need not be mutually exclusive, although in terms of understanding the action research literature they need to be recognized as part of a continuing debate.

Educational action research, as it is generally perceived and practised in Britain, could be defined as a form of self-reflective enquiry whereby practitioners, individually or collaboratively, engage in a critical and systematic examination of their practice in order to generate and develop their own professional knowledge base. It embodies a distinct conception of professional development in that it is assumed that the process of critical reflection enhances the professional understanding of practitioners and, simultaneously, improves the quality of their actions.

However defined, the power of action research lies in its potential for integrating, and examining holistically, key elements of educational practice, including teaching and learning, evaluation and accountability, curriculum development, teacher development and research. Nowhere is this more apparent that in the ideas and work of Lawrence Stenhouse. It has been claimed that the action research movement in Britain can be traced to his formative influence (Elliott, 1981). It seems logical therefore that an examination of action research should begin with a synthesis of his work. Significantly, Stenhouse developed and tested his ideas through the practical involvement in curriculum development projects, unlike a number of influential contemporary theorists whose ideas have been generated independent of, and are considered a priori to, educational practice.

Following Peters (1966), Stenhouse (1975) claims that 'aims' in educational discourse define values and standards intrinsic to the process of education, and not its extrinsic outcomes. Consequently, and contrary to the conventional wisdom of the time, he argues that in planning a curriculum aims should be specified as procedural criteria or principles, rather than translated into behavioural learning objectives. This conviction forms the basis of his process model of curriculum and found practical expression in the Humanities Curriculum Project (HCP) which he directed. By defining the aims of HCP in terms of pedagogical principles, Stenhouse and his team provided a framework for testing and developing educational ideas in action. He envisaged teachers, as the central agents in this enterprise, engaging in a critical and systematic examination of their practice. Put simply, in his own words, the research model of curriculum is 'the evaluative response to the process model' (op.cit., p. 123). Curriculum development of any quality, he claimed, depended on teachers adopting a research stance to practice, implying a particular kind of professionalism. This he termed 'research-based teaching' (op.cit., p. 141). Although it may appear otherwise, Stenhouse is not averse to the idea of the centrally developed curriculum project. For him it is teachers' disposition to an enquiry stance rather than the site of development that determines whether an innovation brings about substantive change in practice.

Stenhouse (1980, 1984) uses 'the artist' as a central metaphor for articulating his conception of the teacher as researcher. Teaching, he claims, is an art 'with the implication that artists exercise autonomy of judgment founded upon research directed towards the improvement of their art' (Stenhouse, 1984, p. 72). In accordance with this conception of teaching, the curriculum is seen as the medium through which teachers develop their art. Consequently the curriculum is inevitably in a state of constant transformation in that 'the process of developing one's art as a teacher . . . is a dialectic of idea and practice not to be separated from change' (Stenhouse, 1980, p. 42). Professional development and curriculum development are part and parcel of the same process, but contingent upon teachers adopting an experimental and investigatory approach to practice.

It is important to realize that Stenhouse's conception of the teacher as researcher is a consequence of, as well as a response to, a particular view of teaching and learning, as expressed in his articulation of research-based teaching. For Stenhouse (1984), education is not learning of the truth: it is 'learning in the context of a search for truth' (op.cit., p. 68). Yet, at all age levels, learners engage with knowledge detached from an understanding of the processes through which it is generated. As such, they become dependent on the authority of teachers, rather than their own independent reasoning, as a source of truth. For Stenhouse the art of teaching is to represent to learners meanings about knowledge rather than to transmit to them the inert products of thinking. They should be given 'access to insights into the status of what they learn' (Stenhouse, 1984, p. 70). Education should enable learners to gain an appreciation of the contestability and provisionality of knowledge for 'security in uncertainty is the armour which a speculative education can offer' (op.cit., p. 188). Elliott (1991, p. 142), commenting on Stenhouse's work, states that 'an educationally worthwhile process involves a reflexive attitude towards the nature of knowledge, on the part of both the teacher and students'. This implies that the crucial question to ask of a curriculum is not what knowledge it should transmit but how knowledge, as the medium of learning through social interaction, should be engaged with and treated. Furthermore, it implies that action research is not something teachers do *on*, or even *for*, their practice; it is what they do *as* their practice. For, if educational values are realized in the teaching/learning process itself rather than through its extrinsic products, a curriculum should of necessity be hypothetical and contestable: therein lies its educative potential for both learners and teachers. As Stenhouse (1983b, p. 192), puts it, 'The teacher who founds his practice of teaching upon research must adopt a research stance to his [*sic*] own practice: it must be provisional and exploratory'.

Following his involvement with Stenhouse in the Humanities Curriculum Project, John Elliott, with a grant from the Ford Foundation, set up in 1973 an action research project to explore and promote discovery/inquiry approaches to teaching. The design of the project originated in the work of HCP. Many teachers involved in this project had been sympathetic to its ideals and principles but experienced considerable difficulties realizing them in practice. The Ford Teaching Project endeavoured to identify the nature of the problems encountered by teachers adopting discovery/inquiry methods with a view to bridging the gap between aspiration and performance.

The findings of the project were cautiously optimistic. The project team felt optimistic about the capacity of the majority of teachers for self-criticism. It was found that the greater the ability of a teacher to self-monitor his/her classroom practice the greater the likelihood of fundamental changes occurring in it. It demonstrated the process by which theory developed empirically through communication between teachers and the project team. Through reflection on practice, teachers were able to generate quite sophisticated theoretical frameworks. Evidence suggested, not surprisingly, that in practice the fostering of autonomous reasoning was incompatible with the prespecification of learning outcomes. Finally, the findings led to the conviction that when reflecting on practice the majority of teachers needed the assistance of a disengaged person to 'mirror' their actions.

A direct consequence of the Ford Teaching Project was the setting up of the Classroom Action Research Network (CARN) in 1976 to support the work of individuals and groups, in Britain and abroad, committed to action research. It is, perhaps, a testimony to the efficacy and appeal of action research that CARN, with few resources apart from the enthusiasm and commitment of its members, has endured the educational turbulence of the 1980s and, indeed, continues to flourish.

A number of action research theorists have developed their ideas within a neo-Aristotelean ethical tradition (Elliott, 1983; Carr and Kemmis, 1986; Grundy, 1987). Aristotle in his *Nicomachean Ethics*, claims that every human action and choice aims at some end or good. He distinguishes between action which is directed towards the making of a product (*poiesis or poietike*), and action which is concerned with doing something well (*praxis*). *Poiesis*, or technical action, is dependent upon the exercise of skill (*techne*) and is informed by a guiding blueprint (*eidos*). *Techne*, as a form of technical reasoning, produces action which accords with established rules; it provides the means to achieving a specific predetermined end (Grundy, 1987). *Praxis* or 'practice' is guided by practical wisdom (*phronesis*), 'a moral disposition to act truly and justly' (Carr and Kemmis, 1986), in the pursuit of ethical values and ideals derived from a conception of the good. Practical wisdom is grounded in experience and, in the light of a conception of the good, enables individuals to choose an appropriate course of action. Practical wisdom is an intellectual virtue as opposed to a moral virtue but is also constitutive of the latter. Moral virtue enables humans to choose the right ends, practical wisdom enables them to choose the right means.

This Aristotelean ethical tradition is explicit in Elliott's (1983) conception of action research. The practical knowledge of teaching, he argues, is 'knowing how' and is based on experience. This tacit practical knowledge constitutes a tradition. Once sufficient mastery of the tradition has been achieved teachers become autonomous professionals in that they have the means to evaluate their own practices. This is the kind of self-evaluation teachers engage in all the time, but it does not help them develop their practical knowledge beyond that which they already possess. Further development is contingent upon teachers being presented with a problem or issue that cannot be solved with their existing practical knowledge and, therefore, requires 'novel and innovatory response' (op.cit., p. 236). In such situations 'some form of conscious reflection and investigation is necessary' (ibid.).

Elliott advocates a form of reflective inquiry based on Aristotle's conception of deliberation. According to Aristotle, we deliberate about those effects produced by our agency but for which the right course of action is not clearly defined. Deliberation is not appropriate or necessary when it is possible to choose the means to ends by appeal to precise rules. Educational practice is an informed, purposive activity directed to the realization of intrinsic ends that cannot be perfectly understood – and hence stated with precision – in advance of, and independent of, chosen means. Thus conceived, it is 'an object of deliberation rather than technical control' (op.cit., p. 232). As deliberation involves the exercise of personal judgement, and the outcomes are always provisional, it is guided by ethical rather than technical rules. In Elliott's view, the capacity of teachers to engage in this kind of deliberative self-evaluation is a necessary condition for their development 'beyond mastery'.

Elliott claims that 'deliberation involves reflecting on ends and means jointly' (op.cit., p. 235). This stands in marked contradiction to Aristotle's unequivocal view that 'we deliberate not about ends but about means' (1955). Indeed, he goes on to argue that as deliberation is concerned with what is practicable for the agent its object 'cannot be the end, but *must* be the means to ends' (op.cit., p. 121, emphasis added). Elliott, however, claims that in the act of deliberating on the choice of a course of action, and then reflecting on its implementation, an understanding of the ends is deepened. In Aristotelean terms, education is an activity which involves *doing* something well, as opposed to the *making* of a product. Its ends, therefore, are intrinsic and cannot logically be separated from means. The relationship is dialectical. As Elliott puts it, 'understanding of means and end develops together through cycles of deliberation and action. In this way professional traditions evolve and change rather than remain static' (op.cit., p. 235).

The tradition of action research represented by Elliott has been criticized by an alternative school of thought (Carr and Kemmis 1986;

Grundy, 1987) which draws upon the writings of critical theorists, notably Habermas, as the basis of a conception of emancipatory action research. This they contrast with practical action research. Emancipatory action research is based on the assumption that teachers' self-understandings of their practices are ideologically distorted and the practices themselves impeded, if not determined, by structural and political constraints. Thus, a major priority of action research is to help teachers recognize the structural and ideological constraints that impinge on their thoughts and actions. As Giddens (1985, p. 126), commenting on the work of Habermas, claims, 'the more human beings understand about the springs of their own behaviour, and the social institutions in which that behaviour is involved, the more they are likely to be able to escape from constraints to which previously they were subject'. However, as teachers' self-understandings of their practices are ideological distortions, they cannot provide an adequate basis for the pursuit of enlightenment and emancipation. For critical theorists the critique of ideology is contingent upon understandings generated by critical social science. Enlightenment comes not through reflection on practice but through reflection on practice in the light of critical social theorems (Grundy, 1987).

Drawing on Gadamer's hermeneutics, Elliott rejects the need to import externally generated theory into the action research process. He argues that critical self-reflection and emancipatory action can be generated from teachers' self-understandings of their practices. This, he claims, renders false the distinction drawn between practical and emancipatory paradigms of action research. Tripp (1990) lends empirical support to Elliott's position. His research suggests that teachers tend, initially, to reflect on the immediate problems of their practice but 'find socially critical questions emerge as they proceed' (op.cit., p. 164). Thus, reflection on practice enables teachers 'to formulate and act upon their own concerns' (op.cit., p. 165), thereby developing themselves professionally, but has the further potential of awakening them to the constraints that impinge on their practices and to the broader social effects of their practice in terms of justice and equality. Consequently, he argues:

> socially critical action research does not necessitate a totally different kind of project from a practical one at the outset; it is more a matter of incorporating into a practical one an understanding of its social context and social effect, and acting upon that context and those effects to facilitate forms of consciousness and practice

that would not have been available within the initial situation or practice

(op.cit., p. 163–4)

This process seems to accord with Elliott's notion of 'consciousness raising' and is probably more a consequence of dialogue with an external consultant than engagement with critical theorems. However, both schools of thought agree on the need for action research to be a collaborative enterprise. Simons (1987) and Elliott (1983) highlight the difficulties experienced by teachers trying to address whole school issues without a supportive organizational structure. Bureaucratically organized institutions are not conducive to collective inquiry. Advocates of action research believe that to bring about substantive change it must involve collective action. It should be an on-going process of deliberation, investigation and dialogue carried out within non-hierarchical, open and participatory management structures. The micropolitical perspective of change suggests, perhaps, that this aspiration may contain more than an element of wishful thinking.

As we noted in Chapter 2, Schon argues that in the face of exponential change it is necessary for institutions to develop as learning systems capable of bringing about their own transformation. Rogers (1983, p. 104) makes a similar point. He argues that the 'goal of education, if we are to survive, is the facilitation of change and learning'. Despite the inherent difficulties, educational institutions engaged in action research are learning systems *par excellence*. Moreover, action research itself, as a form of social practice, demonstrates a propensity to self-transformation in terms of both theory and method and an ability to respond to new agendas as they emerge (Edwards and Rideout, 1991).

## SCHOOL SELF-EVALUATION AND SCHOOL-BASED REVIEW

The terms school self-evaluation and school-based review are virtually synonymous and used generically refer to a plethora of school-level evaluation processes, procedures and schemes. A number of these initiatives originated in the 1970s, in response to the mounting demands for educational accountability. Prominent among these were school self-evaluation schemes initiated by local education authorities (LEAs). The DES Circular 14/77 had provided a sharp reminder to LEAs regarding their curricular responsibilities, including monitoring and evaluation. In a time of diminishing financial resources, school self-evaluation offered LEAs the least costly and, confronted with a tradition of teacher autonomy, the most acceptable way of monitoring the work of their schools. Beginning with the Inner London Education Authority's 'Keeping the School Under Review', the initiative spread rapidly and by the early 1980s at least 80% of the LEAs in England and Wales had adopted some kind of policy for school self-evaluation (Edwards, 1982).

The schemes themselves showed considerable variation in terms of procedure and outcome. For example, some authorities advised schools to produce a written report; in others it was mandatory. However, they embodied a number of common features. The legitimating rhetoric of the schemes advocated power-sharing and joint responsibility, both within the schools and within the local authority. But the schemes themselves conveyed a contrary view. They were devised largely by administrators or advisers. If teachers participated, it was usually headteachers; there was little evidence of 'grass roots' involvement. The most common format was a checklist of questions against which teachers individually and schools collectively were expected to self-evaluate. The questions were riddled with value judgements about the nature and purpose of schooling. The procedures the schemes advocated were largely top-down; they assumed hierarchical structures. Self-evaluation was to be conducted within prevailing organizational and curricular structures. The majority of the schemes assumed an objectives model of curriculum planning, some in explicitly behavioural terms. Schools in Solihull, for example, were encouraged to express their objectives in measurable learning outcomes to be attained within a specified time limit. Thus, the schemes contributed, covertly, to the maintenance of the status quo and reinforced rather than challenged a technicist view of curriculum.

There is little research evidence available to suggest that these schemes had any lasting, or even short-term, impact on schools in general or, conversely, that they did not. However, from what is known about schools it seems reasonable to assume that in many the implementation of the scheme would have resulted in little more than the dusting down, and token updating, of the 'aims and objectives' document or, perhaps, an overhaul of the curricular structure. There was no requirement for teachers to engage in any inquiry beyond the staffroom door. It is doubtful, therefore, that they activated teachers, individually or collectively, to engage in a systematic, critical and sustained examination of their classroom practices. Simons (1987) attributes LEAs' 'hasty resort to checklists' as a response to account-ability pressures. Whatever the motives, the belief that schools could change through such an approach was, with hindsight, somewhat naive.

It would be misleading to imply that the LEA schemes, as described above, are representative of school self-evaluation *per se*, for many schools and some LEAs have adopted a more action research-oriented approach. And, in response to the deficiencies inherent in the LEA schemes, other forms of institutional self-evaluation have been developed. In Britain the most notable, and most widely used, is GRIDS (Guidelines for Review and Institutional Development). Other well-documented approaches of a similar genre include organization development (OD), the Organisation for Economic Co-operation and Development (OECD) sponsored International School Improvement Project (ISIP), the Institutional Development Programme (IDP) developed by the Norwegian-based International Movements Towards Educational Change (IMTEC) and the Diagnosis of Individual and Organizational Needs (DION).

GRIDS originated in 1981 as a Schools Council project in conjunction with, and based at, the University of Bristol. Sponsorship for its second stage was provided by the Schools Curriculum Development Committee which had been set up in 1982 to replace the Schools Council. Unlike many of the LEA self-evaluation schemes, GRIDS was designed specifically to promote school development rather than to fulfil any accountability function (Reid, Hopkins and Holly, 1987).

We believe, on a number of counts, that GRIDS has conceptual and methodological deficiencies which limit its potential to promote educational change. Although claiming otherwise, it clearly embodies a mechanistic and somewhat simplistic view of change, in keeping with the technological perspective we discussed in Chapter 2. It draws on work done in the field of organization development, an approach underpinned by behavioural theory and which views individuals 'primarily as functional units within the system' (Hord, 1987). GRIDS, as described in the handbooks, is essentially a structured, five-stage, linear process of review and development. Each stage is broken down into a number of steps, nineteen in total. Adherence to the systematic step-by-step approach is recommended throughout (Hopkins, 1990). Data are gathered using a survey sheet that is given to all staff during the initial review stage. This, it is claimed, gives the teacher an opportunity to state individually and anonymously what he/she feels are the priority areas for development (Hopkins, op.cit.). But, while subscribing to the democratic principles of collaboration and consultation, the procedures recommended by GRIDS assume hierarchical organizational structures and assume the overall control and direction of the review is to remain firmly in the hands of the head or senior management. Emphasis is placed on the school as a functioning organization rather than on its central educative purposes as expressed in and through the curriculum. These are perceived to be of secondary concern. A degree of homogeneity and consensus is assumed which belies the political realities of schools as demonstrated through research (Richardson, 1973; Ball, 1981; Dalton, 1988).

The premise of GRIDS is that 'development follows from review' (Hopkins, 1990, p. 123) This contrasts with the premise of action research which envisages review and development as integral parts of the same process, where, in Stenhouse's (1975, p. 124) terms, 'conjectures and refutations are woven into one logic'. In GRIDS the relationship between review and development is under-theorized. It is assumed that once review has been undertaken development will follow as night follows day. This is clearly not the case as the designers of GRIDS and similar schemes have subsequently found. Further questions have been raised concerning an 'apparent lack of rigour and objectivity in many review and development procedures' (Hopkins, 1990, p. 125). As Holly (1984, p. 14), a member of the GRIDS team, comments, 'teachers involved in GRIDS projects have found it difficult to judge the effectiveness and quality of their practice'. Consequently 'It often fails to lead to "institutional change". . . it succeeds only in "tinkering" at the organizational edges' (ibid.).

The GRIDS materials are described as 'a do-it-yourself kit for review and development' (McMahon *et al.*, 1984). Perhaps this is a more revealing analogy than originally intended. There is of course the usual disclaimer that schools can adapt the materials to suit their own institutional needs. Furthermore, it has also been argued that GRIDS provides a starting point and that, once a commitment to evaluation is established, schools will develop their own more sophisticated approaches. Even if this is the case, and we consider it unlikely, it should not detract from its conceptual and methodological shortcomings. The impact that GRIDS has when practised is difficult to determine. The reports that are available tend to be 'exhortatory' or 'rhetorical' and written from a management perspective. Little recorded evidence is available of its consequences at the 'grass roots' level of classroom practice.

We are not alone in criticizing GRIDS and similar technocratic schemes. Holt (1987, p. 50) in relation to OD comments: 'OD amounts to a systems approach, in which the individual is subordinate to the group, and the ends and means are seen as separate and noninteracting: all that is needed to ensure operational effectiveness is clarity about goals and the necessary repertoire of free-standing skills to implement them'.

An understanding of the school self-evaluation movement provides a useful basis for analysing a number of current educational issues, including an opportunity to rethink the relationship between review and development. In accordance with the 1988 Education Reform Act, schools are now legally required to produce a school development plan. These could become, on the one hand, a manipulative, managerial strategy for maintaining the status quo or, on the other, a means for promoting genuine participatory forms of school management. Similarly, they could provide the basis for bringing about institutionally desired change or used for the uncritical implementation of externally directed policy. Yet again, they could be directed towards the bureaucratic needs of the school as an organization or towards the needs of the school as a learning community. It is difficult to generalize, but there is evidence to suggest that at present the design of school development plans is being influenced overtly by technicist assumptions as found in schemes such as GRIDS and OD. Some LEAs have prescribed a model to which all schools will be expected to conform. On the other hand, LEAs such as Leicestershire have allowed, indeed encouraged, each school to exercise a considerable degree of autonomy in constructing their own development plan but with the proviso that curriculum review should be the central focus.

An alternative version of school self-evaluation is that put forward by Holt (1987) which draws largely on the work of the neo-Aristoteleans Joseph Schwab and Alasdair MacIntyre. This Holt terms school-focused deliberation and it has much in common with Elliott's notion of deliberative self-evaluation, as previously described. Indeed, Elliott (1988, 1991) himself has incorporated the ideas of MacIntyre (1985) into his recent work. The common thread in Holt's (1987, p. 131) argument is that 'educational change involves moral judgments and educational planning implies applying values to a practical activity'.

Through the work of MacIntyre, Holt relates his ideas to the Aristotelean ethical tradition. Central to this tradition is the exercise of the virtues. The virtues are qualities, moral and intellectual, the possession of which enable individuals not only to achieve the good but also to increase both their self-knowledge and their knowledge of the good. It is in practices, in the pursuit of goods internal to those practices, that the virtues are exercised.

MacIntyre describes a practice as

> any coherent and complex form of socially established cooperative human activity through which goods internal to that form of activity are realized in the course of trying to achieve those standards of excellence which are appropriate to, and partially definitive of that activity, with the result that human powers to achieve excellence, and human conceptions of the ends and goods involved are systematically extended.
>
> (MacIntyre, 1985, p. 187)

Practices, MacIntyre argues, are sustained by institutions and transmitted and reshaped through traditions. As the goods internal to a practice are contestable, and change during the history of the practice, traditions will inevitably conflict. He claims:

> A living tradition . . . is a historically extended socially embodied argument, and an argument precisely in part about the goods which constitute that tradition. . . . The history of a practice in our time is generally and characteristically embedded in and made intelligible in terms of the larger and longer history of the tradition through which the practice in its present form was conveyed to us.
>
> (op.cit., p. 222)

This has important implications in that it adds weight to the argument for those sociohistorical approaches to curriculum studies as advocated by Goodson, which we explored in Chapter 2. It implies that educational practitioners cannot exercise virtues in pursuit of goods internal to the practice in which they engage unless they have some understanding of the tradition in which that practice is located. For, as MacIntyre argues (op.cit., p. 221), 'insofar as the virtues sustain the relationships required for practices, they have to sustain relationships to the past – and to the future – as well as to the present'.

This suggests that all forms of reflective inquiry should aim at developing in teachers both a greater understanding of their current practices and a deeper insight into the ways in which those practices, and themselves as practitioners, are historically and socially constituted.

# SUMMARY AND CONCLUSIONS

On the basis of available evidence, the capacity of school self-evaluation or school-based review to bring about substantive change, that is change which challenges the deeper structures and categorical meanings of schooling, has to be questioned. However, there is evidence to suggest that some forms of practitioner inquiry have achieved notable gains in promoting both teacher and curriculum development. Moreover, it is perhaps the democratic principles to which these forms of inquiry aspire, rather than their efficacy to bring about change, that provide the source of their legitimation. In the light of what is known about factors which inhibit the process of change, any success, however small, has to be acknowledged as significant.

The implementation of a centrally prescribed curriculum in England and Wales raises important questions about the future of school-centred innovation in general and reflective forms of evaluation, such as action research, in particular. For example, a centrally prescribed curriculum is incompatible with Stenhouse's conception of research-based teaching being the means through which teachers develop their art. For, as he points out, 'Truth cannot be defined by the state even through democratic processes: close control of curricula and teaching methods in schools is to be likened to the totalitarian control of art' (1984, p. 68).

Action research is not about the instrumentality of action. It is concerned, primarily, with questions of meaning and value and, as van Manen points out, these questions cannot be solved and done away with; 'they can only be better or more deeply understood' (1990, p. 155). In the implementation of a centrally prescribed curriculum we need to be vigilant lest, in the words of van Manen (ibid.), 'action research too easily slips from thoughtful reflection on experience into a rationality of problem thinking and problem solving'.

Furthermore, we saw in Chapter 3 that the strategies for implementing this centrally prescribed curriculum deliberately seek to exclude teachers from reflection on its merits or value at this level, or at least from acting on such reflection, a facility which is essential to action research, however this might be conceived, and to all forms of school-centred innovation. We saw also that, conversely, the imposition of this kind of curriculum must be undertaken by means which are largely power-coercive. It is of enormous advantage, therefore, to those seeking to establish this curriculum not merely to disallow action based on this kind of teacher reflection but, further, to discourage such reflection from occurring in the first place. A major device for achieving this goal, a significant aspect of the power-coercive strategies currently being employed, is the skilful use of rhetoric. It is to a consideration of this that we turn in Chapter 5.

# 5

# CURRICULUM CHANGE AND EDUCATIONAL DISCOURSE

Our discussion of the concept of change in Chapter 1 revealed not only that it is possible to conceive of change, and thus to respond to it, in several different ways but also that the way in which we conceive of and respond to it will have important implications for our view of knowledge, educational practice and the very nature of society. In particular, a rationalist view of change as an inevitable process of movement from or to some state of perfection will be based on a Newtonian knowledge-paradigm, will lead to approaches to education which emphasize the transmission of knowledge and/or the attainment of prestated 'aims and objectives' and will only make sense if matched by some form of totalitarian political organization. By contrast, an empiricist or pragmatist view of change as 'fact', as a feature of human existence to be lived with and adapted to, will be based on a 'post-modern' knowledge-paradigm, will encourage a stress in educational planning on the processes of individual growth and development, and will require a democratic social structure as its proper context. It may be further noted that there is an inevitable conceptual interconnection between these theoretical positions: rationalism > Newtonian knowledge-paradigm > curriculum as content and/or as product > totalitarianism; and empiricism/pragmatism > 'post-modern' knowledge-paradigm > curriculum as process > democracy; so that decisions in any of these dimensions must bring with them implications for the others. In particular, an emphasis on the curriculum as a device for the transmission of predetermined knowledge must have implications for individual freedom and bear suggestions of totalitarianism (which is why, incidentally, the notion of a national curriculum was regarded as unacceptable in the United Kingdom in the 1930s). Conversely, commitment to democratic forms of social living must imply acceptance of curriculum as process, as John Dewey made plain.

Subsequent chapters have reinforced the points made in Chapter 1. They have revealed how important it is to recognize the human dimension of education and thus of educational change, to acknowledge, within a democratic context, the unique individuality not only of every pupil but also of every teacher and every school. It will have become apparent, both from our exploration of theories of change in Chapter 2 and our review in Chapters 3 and 4 of the strategies and mechanisms which have been adopted for the implementation of change, that the only basis for change which is anything other than cosmetic and superficial is one which takes account of the individual characteristics of all those affected by it.

It will also be clear that none of these insights is reflected in the processes currently in train for the establishment of the National Curriculum in the United Kingdom and the dramatic changes in the curriculum, especially that of primary schools, and even more especially that of nursery/infant or first schools, which this entails. For those processes are taking us back to attempts to change the curriculum through the creation of national agencies, the inadequacies of which we highlighted in Chapter 3; they are taking us away from the subtleties of school-based initiatives which we explored in Chapter 4; and they are ignoring all of the theoretical perspectives we outlined in Chapter 2.

All of those discussions, however, would seem to indicate, first, that these processes are unlikely to be effective in any real, deep or genuine sense, that whatever changes they bring about are likely to be superficial and to be implemented by teachers in a somewhat mechanistic manner. Second, the manifest failure of attempts at curriculum change on a national scale which have sought to adopt empirical–rational or normative–re-educative approaches (Bennis, Benne and Chin, 1969) to persuade teachers of their value must suggest that, if the changes associated with the National Curriculum are to be effectively imposed on schools, the devices adopted to achieve this must be of a power-coercive kind. One such device, of course, as we have seen, is the enshrinement of that National Curriculum in the legal structures of an Education Act; a second is the creation of a system of testing of all pupils at four 'key-stages' in their educational careers – perhaps the most effective means of ensuring that schools concentrate on those National Curriculum attainment targets which will be the subject of such tests. A third, and more subtle, device is the massive use of rhetoric in the official documentation which seeks not only to advise teachers on the implementation of the National Curriculum but also to ensure their acceptance of it. If such documentation demonstrated an attempt to offer rational argument in support of these changes, then of course we would have to recognize it as an attempt at empirical–rational or normative–re-educative tactics. Such approaches, however, are not available to those seeking to sell to teachers a curriculum which is so obviously flawed (Lawton, 1987) and which flies so blatantly in the face of so many aspects of current professional understanding (Kelly, 1990) as to be impossible to establish by any devices other than those of a power-coercive kind.

Power-coercive strategies, however, are increasingly difficult to adopt or employ, unless one does so in the most subtle of ways. And one of the subtlest ways in which one can attempt to do this is by the use of rhetoric and, especially, by the legitimation of discourse. If one can by these devices change the ways in which teachers and others view education and schooling and, more importantly, the ways in which they discuss and talk about education and schooling, then one can deflect and control also their ways of thinking about education and schooling – not by rational argument but by manipulation of their thought processes. In education, therefore, as in all areas of society, we are now continuously subject to government by rhetoric. We are almost a decade beyond 1984; and we would do well not to lose sight of that fact.

Interest in the issue of the language of educational discourse has increased significantly in recent times. A major reason for this must be the growing concern about the level and quality of current pronouncements and publications on educational policy. The parameters of the educational debate have been progressively narrowed, and that debate has been characterized by not only a lack of, but also a lack of concern for, conceptual clarity. This in turn has been associated with an escalation of the use of rhetoric in these pronouncements and publications, not only by politicians but also by those whose task it is to implement the policies of those politicians. As a consequence of these developments there has emerged an awareness that educational discourse is being manipulated to achieve political ends, that it is becoming a device for the control of education, and even the repression of challenge to political policies, rather than the vehicle for free and open discussion in the interests of continued development and change, that the intellectual and social context of educational practice is shifting, indeed being shifted, from democracy to an incipient form of totalitarianism, of a kind that matches the content-based form of National Curriculum which has now been established in the United Kingdom and the view of knowledge upon which it is based.

This chapter sets out to explore this question, to look at some aspects of the current debate about education and curriculum issues in some detail, in order to try to establish whether there are any grounds for this kind of concern, to discover where and how these features manifest themselves and to identify ways in which their inhibiting and limiting effects may be minimized or even obviated. It will do this by first considering the use of rhetoric, what it is, the linguistic devices it employs – especially its use of metaphor and its deliberate obfuscation of conceptual and logical distinctions – and where, when and, indeed, if its use is justified. Second, it will explore the recent and developing debate about the legitimation of discourse, the ways in which forms of discourse become established and legitimated, and especially attempts at political control of these forms of discourse. Finally, in so doing, it will review the current intellectual climate in relation to educational theory and practice in the United Kingdom against the background of the perspectives the earlier discussion will have established. In short, it will examine the issue of the relationship between change in educational practice and change in educational discourse.

## RHETORIC

Rhetoric was once regarded as an essential element in a 'liberal education' or in the education of a gentleman, i.e. someone whose main task in life it would be to control and govern others. It was a major part of the training of an orator, described by the Roman philosopher Cato as 'a good man skilled in the art of speaking'. This was the art to which all educated men [*sic*] aspired. Thus it was part of the Roman Quintilian's *trivium* (a strange combination of grammar, rhetoric and logic or dialectic) which along with the *quadrivium* (music, arithmetic, geometry and astronomy – note the influence of Plato) constituted what was seen in Roman times as a 'liberal education', and which was reiterated in the 16th century, after the rediscovery of Quintilian's *Institutes*, by writers such as Thomas Elyot.

It may be claimed that the term 'rhetoric' had a different connotation in those times from that, largely pejorative, meaning it bears now. However, the art of oratory has ever been to persuade and influence through choice of 'honeyed words' rather than through reasoned argument, and to achieve one's purposes, whatever these might be, rather than to seek fearlessly after 'the truth'. We should note that in Greek and Roman times oratory was the main ingredient of the administration of legal justice as well as of political debate and activity, so that in both of these major areas of public life the art of public speaking was the most important attribute of the person who wished to succeed. Perhaps, then, it is not the concept of rhetoric which has changed but merely our attitude towards it.

However, it is now recognized as the deliberate use of language to influence the attitudes and values of others, to persuade by devices other than rational argument, to obfuscate realities; and, in order to do this, it must seek to inhibit and discourage free and open debate or discourse. It thus belongs in the totalitarian rather than the democratic version of the scenarios we painted earlier. In the context of education, it belongs to, and certainly leads to, a closed rather than an open system, and is predicated on a knowledge-paradigm which is rationalist and Newtonian.

There are several major devices which it uses to achieve its goals, and it is worth noting here that, as the legitimacy of rhetoric itself has come to be questioned and challenged, its answer has been to develop these devices to higher levels of subtlety and sophistication, in order, especially, to conceal them from detection. We must now look at the more obvious of these devices in some detail.

## The blurring of logical distinctions

It is important for clarity of thinking and for coherence of debate and discussion that we recognize the logical status of the assertions or utterances which are being made, both by ourselves and by others. In broad, and perhaps somewhat simplified terms, there are three logically quite distinct forms of assertion or utterance. First, there are straightforward *factual* or empirical assertions, of a kind whose truth or validity is determined by reference to the evidence of empirically observable events. Thus, if I assert that 'the cat is on the mat', whether this is true or not is to be decided on the visible evidence – or lack of it. These are utterances which philosophers have called 'synthetic *a posteriori* propositions' – synthetic because they link together two quite discrete objects or concepts (in the example given 'cat' and 'mat') and *a posteriori* because they are dependent on experience for their verification. Another way of looking at this is to consider not assertions but questions, and the kind of answer the question is seeking or the kind of evidence which would be appropriate to answering it. Thus

John Wilson (1963 p. 2) offers the example of 'Is a whale able to sink a 15,000 ton liner?' and indicates that this is a question of fact: 'to be in a position to answer it, all we have to do is to find out the relevant facts' (ibid.).

Second, we have assertions or questions which are of a quite different logical status; they are *conceptual*. The assertion that 'triangles have three sides' tells us something about the meaning of the word 'triangle', about the concept of 'triangle', rather than about the world of empirical experience. Again to use John Wilson's example (ibid.), the question 'Is a whale a fish?' is posing a conceptual rather than an empirical issue; it is a question of definition, of meaning, of concept, and, to answer it, we need to explore not the world of experience but our use of language and the *meanings* that words and concepts bear in our language. 'What we want to know is what we normally mean by "fish", how one verifies whether something is a fish or not, what *counts* (author's emphasis) as a fish' (op.cit., p. 4). Such assertions are those philosophers have called 'analytic *a priori* propositions', i.e. they are not synthetic in the sense of putting two quite discrete objects or concepts together; they are 'analytic' in the sense of offering us an analysis or a definition of a term or a concept; and they are *a priori* in the literal sense of being independent of experience.

Third, we must note that some utterances are assertions of *value*. They are neither empirical nor conceptual. Thus, if we assert that 'telling lies is wrong' or that '*Hamlet* is a great play' or that 'communism (or capitalism or democracy) is the best political system', or if we express these as questions, 'Is telling lies wrong?', 'Is *Hamlet* a great play?', 'Is communism (or capitalism or democracy) the best political system?', we are raising issues which are neither matters of fact nor matters of meaning or concept; they are assertions of value (or questions about value) – prescriptions rather than descriptions – and thus lend themselves to verification neither by a search for relevant evidence nor by an analysis of language or meaning. Indeed, their logical status has been much debated and it has even been argued that they are not proper utterances or even proper questions at all. They are what philosophers have called 'synthetic *a priori* propositions' – not analytic, but also not dependent on experience, and thus highly problematic. Fortunately, we need not pursue that debate here. What we must note, however, and indeed stress, is that they represent a third kind of assertion, utterance or question, and that they must be handled differently from the other two.

A further aspect of this which we must note, and one which offers the purveyor of rhetoric a major device, is that *grammatically* all of these utterances are identical. Consider these three assertions:

(1) At all times, whether in streamed or non-streamed schools, academic standards are related to age.

(Barker-Lunn, 1970, p. 101)

(2) The planning of a process-based curriculum begins with a statement of the procedural principles upon which it is to be implemented.

(3) Intrinsically worthwhile activities are those with a high cognitive content.

On the surface, all of those assertions appear to be the same. A closer look, however, reveals that they are only the same *grammatically*; *logically* they are very different.

And, if, like John Wilson, we concern ourselves with questions rather than with assertions, we find the same characteristics and the same potential problems. He invites us (1963, p. 7) to consider these three questions:

(1) Is communism likely to spread all over the world?
(2) Is communism a desirable system of government?
(3) Is communism compatible with democracy?

Again, the grammar suggests that these questions are alike. Again, closer analysis reveals essential differences, differences of a kind which must lead us to deal with and respond to them quite differently.

This feature of language, while adding richness and providing much scope to those, like poets and novelists, whose task it is to use language creatively and imaginatively, offers vast possibilities for logical and conceptual confusion, since we can very easily slip into muddling these categories in our own thinking and in debate with others. It also offers wide-ranging opportunities to those who wish to use language to create deliberate confusion, to mislead us, to influence our attitudes or to persuade us into certain decisions or actions without recourse to rational argument. It is thus a major rhetorical device.

Consider, for example, the following 'statements':

A curriculum which meets these general criteria is an entitlement for all pupils.

(DES, 1989a, para. 2.2)

Assessment is an integral part of the National Curriculum.

(op.cit., para. 6.1)

All pupils share the same statutory entitlement to a broad and balanced curriculum, including access to the National Curriculum.

> (op.cit., para. 8.1)

And so on.

One further aspect of this should also be noted. This lack of obvious grammatical distinction between different kinds of assertion also makes it possible to make empirical assertions, those for which evidence should be produced, or at least acknowledged as being necessary, without offering any such evidence at all. The documentation which has emerged from DES, NCC and SEAC in support of the implementation of the National Curriculum in the United Kingdom is littered with such unsubstantiated assertions.

> There is much agreement ... about the subjects which should be included in the secular curriculum for 5–16 year olds; and valuable progress has been made towards securing agreement about the objectives and content of particular subjects.
>
> (DES, 1987, p. 2)

> The imaginative application of professional skills at all levels of the education service, within a statutory framework which sets clear objectives, *will* (author's emphasis) raise standards.
>
> (op.cit., p. 5)

> Cross-curricular themes, including personal and social education, are by their nature rooted in subjects, and where courses are offered they need to be planned and developed in relation to subject teaching.
>
> (DES, 1989b, p. 2)

> There will be a great deal of scope for teachers in schools to carry out curriculum development without cutting across the statutory requirements.
>
> (DES, 1989a, para. 5.4)

> The National Curriculum will offer a broad and balanced education for all pupils providing progression and continuity from 5 to 16 and beyond.
>
> (NCC, 1990, p. 1)

> The National Curriculum ... will be an effective way of ensuring that good curricular practice is much more widely employed.
>
> (DES, 1989a, para. 3.1)

And so on again.

## The use of emotive language

A second major rhetorical device is the use of emotive language – words, expressions, figures of speech, which are known to conjure up certain attitudes and responses, whether positive or negative, in one's audience. Again, this is a device well and appropriately used in literature, where the conjuring up of attitudes and responses is the purpose of the exercise. It is also much beloved of propagandists and of those whose concern is with rhetoric rather than rationality.

It is a well-known feature of language that words gather emotive as well as literal connotations. It was once pointed out at some length (Ryan, 1965), for example, that the suffixes '-less' and '-free', while apparently having the same literal meaning, are used to convey quite different attitudes and to invoke quite different responses. Thus, there is an important difference between care*free* motoring and care*less* motoring; and what may be a meat*free* diet to the vegetarian is meat*less* to the carnivore. Almost every word is a 'pro' or a 'con' word (Nowell-Smith, 1954) – a 'hurrah' or a 'boo' word. Our choice of words thus reflects our attitudes and feelings. It also influences, and can be used to influence, those of others.

It is precisely this feature of language that enables us to manipulate it to our ends. It is common in newspaper reporting, especially in the more popular press, and it is the stock-in-trade of politicians, who never, for example, 'correct an error they have made' but always 'adjust their policies to meet changing circumstances', while their opponents, of course, are always described as doing the opposite. An official report of one civil war once asserted that the rebels 'butchered' all the prisoners they took, while those taken by the government forces were 'summarily executed'.

Again, current political statements on education are littered with 'pro' words in support of the policies they are intended to implement – and often with 'con' words to refer to those policies and practices they are concerned to oust. Thus 'breadth', 'balance', 'entitlement', 'relevance', 'practical', 'progression' (but not 'progress*ive*'), 'continuity', 'coherence', and many more such terms, whose meanings need a good deal more analytical unpacking than they ever receive, are to be found on almost every page of the documentation that has been published in support of the National Curriculum.

Furthermore, one of the most effective and cunning devices to be found in the rhetoric with which the teaching profession is currently being bombarded is the use of 'pro' or 'buzz' words culled from the very discourse it is the concern to oust and replace and from the theories it aims to 'rubbish'. Thus terms like 'process' and 'development', which are central concepts in those learner-centred, personalized theories of, and approaches to, education which current policies are concerned to eliminate, and much of the language associated with school-centred innovation, as we saw in Chapter 4, have been hijacked and are extensively used in propounding the new, replacement policies. The concepts themselves of course are not taken over, since it is the concepts which give offence; merely the terms used. And, when those terms are used, even with quite different meanings, they continue to carry the favourable connotations of the theories they have been stolen from – at least for those (many) people who are less than fully alive to the conceptual subtleties and nuances of language.

## The use of metaphor

A third major device of rhetoric is the use – or misuse – of metaphor. Again we must note that this is an important literary tool, essential to poetry, and indeed to all forms of literature, adding not only linguistic richness and interest, but also enhanced dimensions of meaning. For it uses words and concepts more usually associated with contexts different from that under discussion and thus brings to that discussion added connotations and nuances of meaning. It also does this by taking us beyond the mere factual or by adding subtle variations and new tonalities to the factual. Thus, when Shakespeare makes Hamlet describe life or human existence as 'an unweeded garden', he is offering us far more in the way of meaning as well as imagery than if he had made him say 'life is unpleasant' – and also ensuring immortality for his words.

Again, however, metaphor can be used – or misused – in contexts where it may not be appropriate, where it is designed not to invoke a response but to inhibit and/or control our responses. By the use of metaphor one can seek to introduce ideas, concepts and associations into the minds of one's listeners or readers of a kind intended to influence their attitudes, their values, their thinking, in largely unconscious ways. Thus, throughout the official literature on the National Curriculum, we are offered a commercial/industrial imagery which encourages us to see our schools as factories. Teachers are invited to view their task as one of 'delivering' a 'product'; they are subjected to 'quality-control mechanisms'; they are encouraged to focus their efforts on increased 'productivity', usually at a more 'economic costing' (i.e. on the cheap); inspectors and advisers have in many places acquired new titles as 'quality control' specialists. Soon education will be run, like the Rev Awdry's railway system, by a 'Fat Controller' – if this has not happened already.

Further, we should note that the effectiveness of this particular piece of rhetoric can be gauged by the number of teachers and others in education who now themselves use these terms in discussing their work, with little questioning of the view of education that this imagery reflects and even imposes – a view which, amongst other things, implies a technicist concept of the teacher's role in relation to the curriculum and which thus effectively denies him/her any deeper involvement.

We must note, of course, the emphasis that has been placed in recent academic discussions of the role of metaphor in language on a 'constructionist' view of metaphor (Ortony, 1979). To criticize metaphor, as we are doing here, as an inappropriate rhetorical device is, some would argue, to hanker after a *literal* use of language which is impossible of attainment. Faith in language as a tool for the *objective* characterization of reality has been totally eroded by such developments as psychological views of 'cognition as the result of mental construction' (Ortony, 1979, p. 1), by views of cognition as 'assimilation' and 'accommodation' to one's personal schemata, by notions of meaning as constructed, by phenomenological theories of perception and by the recognition that the human mind will always go beyond the information it receives or is given.

Hence the view has been expressed that metaphor is 'an essential characteristic of the creativity of language' (op.cit., p. 2), that, since our use of language is *essentially* creative, metaphor must be viewed in that light rather than 'as deviant and parasitic upon normal usage' (ibid.). This distinction, as Ortony goes on to stress, reflects 'a more fundamental and pervasive difference of opinion about the relationship between language and the world' (ibid.). A constructionist view of metaphor is concerned to break down the distinction, which we are stressing here, between the metaphorical and the literal, while a non-constructionist view argues that 'metaphors characterize rhetoric, not scientific discourse' (ibid.).

However, it is not necessary to deny the validity of a constructionist view of language and of metaphor in order to criticize the misuse of metaphor as a dangerous rhetorical device. A distinction must be made between the use of language – and metaphor – to create one's own world and to generate one's own meanings and their misuse as forms of rhetoric designed to create those of others. Nor is it to deny a constructionist view to point out the dangers of this use of language and metaphor to manipulate the views, attitudes and values of others. Indeed, it is necessary to recognize the subjectivity of both language and metaphor in order to avoid being misled or manipulated in our own thinking by the language and metaphors of others. We need to appreciate these dangers in order to be able to view the world 'reflexively' (Slaughter, 1989, p. 164), to gain greater control over it and to secure 'greater freedom from ideological and linguistic traps' (ibid.).

## Argument from analogy

Ortony (1979) offers us a further distinction, that between 'microscopic' and 'macroscopic' metaphors – those at the level of single words or sentences ('individual' metaphors) and 'systems of metaphors, or metaphoric models' (op.cit., p. 4), systems or models which become forms of discourse or discursive practice, as we shall see later in this chapter.

The concept of a 'macroscopic' metaphor or a 'metaphoric model' raises a further point that is worth noting about the use of metaphor, a further danger in its use as a rhetorical device. For metaphoric systems encourage argument from analogy; they go beyond the merely illustrative or amplificatory use of metaphor and accept the metaphor as a basis for developing an argument. It is when this happens that the metaphor has become a dangerous rhetorical device.

For example, it is one thing to accept the metaphor of the school as a factory as an illustration, perhaps, of the fact that it needs efficiency of management. It is an unwarranted extension of that analogy, however, to *infer* that schools need the same kinds of management structure as are appropriate to factories, or that their effectiveness is to be evaluated by reference to their 'output', or that quantity of 'throughput' is a further criterion of effectiveness, or that teachers can be seen as 'operatives' and their professional competence judged in relation to their 'productivity', or that, as is currently being urged on university institutions, increased 'throughput' must be accompanied by reduced unit-costs (as it would be in any efficiently run sausage factory).

The fallacy of argument from analogy becomes totally plain if we pursue it by way of a *reductio ad absurdum*. For the factory analogy, if extended, requires us not only to increase the efficiency of our production line, nor only to grade pupils, like eggs, at regular intervals as they pass along it; it also requires us to consider what we are to do with those who turn out to be 'seconds' or even completely unsaleable 'rejects'. Do we attempt to recycle them in some way? Do we throw them on to some scrap-heap? Do we try to pass them off on to an unsuspecting public as genuine products? What would the manager of a sausage factory do in such circumstances? Such questions may seem absurd; if so, they demonstrate the absurdity of the analogy and the fallacy of arguments derived from it. They may seem fanciful; if so, again this reflects on the limitations of the metaphor. If, however, they seem to us to be totally unrelated to the reality of current policies, then we should probably inspect those policies more closely.

The dangers of argument from analogy, and, indeed, of the use of analogy or metaphor itself, will be apparent from these examples. It will also be clear how effective the creation of new forms of discourse or new discursive practices can be in ensuring ease of implementation of one's policies. This is a point we will return to later.

## The justification of the use of rhetoric

At this point we must pause to ask whether the use of rhetoric can ever be appropriate in the context of academic, scholarly or professional discourse.

Rhetoric is – unfortunately, one might add – the very stuff of politics. For politicians, as we saw earlier, are concerned to persuade us of the attractions of their policies and of the consequent necessity of voting for them, and, almost by definition, this is not something they will achieve very easily by reasoned argument. This, again as we saw earlier, is why a training in rhetoric, or at least in the arts of oratory, was once seen as an essential ingredient of a preparation for power and for public life. It might be added that every intelligent citizen expects this of politicians, expects a 'party-line' to be proffered in any public forum rather than a carefully thought-through personal view; and most can, to a greater or lesser degree, recognize and cope with this kind of rhetoric.

It is more disturbing, however, that rhetoric has become the stock-in-trade of those whose task it is to implement government policy, especially in the field of education, where a commitment to reasoned argument might be regarded as a *sine qua non* of any educational enterprise. For the 'educrats' of DES, NCC, SEAC, UFC and the rest, along with Her Majesty's Inspectors, whose role traditionally was to advise government rather than merely to implement government policies, are increasingly recognizing that it is much easier to implement political policies, especially if those policies are in themselves somewhat suspect, by leading teachers and others in the profession to an uncritical acceptance of them by means of the skilful use of rhetoric – choice of words, selection of metaphors, creation of forms of discourse – than by attempting to persuade us by rational argument of the value and merits of the direction in which they are leading us. In short, as we saw earlier, where the nature of the changes being imposed is such as not to lend itself to empirical–rational or normative–re-educative means of implementation, recourse must be had to power-coercive devices, and especially those of a covert and subtle kind.

It is even more disturbing when teachers and others fall for the rhetoric, accept the metaphors and allow themselves to be confined within the new restrictive forms of discourse; often themselves describing former discursive practices and the issues they focused our thinking upon as 'outmoded', 'outdated', 'old hat', and as somehow properly superseded by those current forms which, as we shall soon see, have been artificially created to oust and replace them. It is also most disturbing to find, as one so often does, that the media have been duped and silenced by this process too. For the media should in a democratic society provide a free and open forum for discussion as a counter to this kind of anti-intellectual manipulation.

For our final point about the use of rhetoric to change attitudes, values, policies and/or practices is that it should have no place in a truly democratic society. It is a mild version – perhaps becoming less mild – of those propagandist devices we associate with the fictions of Orwell and Huxley, and with the realities of totalitarian, even fascist, political systems. A democratic society, as we suggested at the beginning of this chapter, should offer scope for, and indeed seek deliberately to create a climate for, free and open debate on all issues, in order to provide a context within which such debate can lead to genuine forms of change, forms of change which result from wide-reaching debate to which all who are affected have ample opportunity to contribute, rather than forms which are generated by one, dominant, section of society, with merely a facade of consultation, imposed by the use of rhetorical devices of all kinds, and maintained by means which offer little scope for that further development – and no scope for the continuous development – which is essential to the health of any society which seeks to be genuinely democratic.

It has become apparent in this discussion of rhetoric and its place in education that a key issue is that of discursive practices and of the legitimation of discourse. It is to this that we now turn in the last major section of this chapter.

## THE LEGITIMATION OF DISCOURSE

We noted earlier that we often hear these days, both from within and outside the teaching profession, that times have changed, that we are in a new era and that the debates of the past are of no relevance to this new era. It is of course true that times have changed and that a new era of educational practice has been entered. It does not follow from that, however, that that new era is necessarily better than the one we have left behind. Neither, therefore, does it follow that we should merely accept it, along with the assumptions upon which it is built, without question or challenge, nor that there is nothing to be gained from comparing the new era with the old to see whether we really believe that it represents a step forward, nor that we should reject out of hand the value of the insights which emerged from the work of those agencies, such as the Schools Council, which did their work at a different time and to a different brief. In all spheres of life, every era has its own fashions and makes its own assumptions, but those fashions and assumptions are there to be challenged and not merely accepted unquestioningly. As Fay Weldon says in a 'letter to Alice',

> I have no doubt, Alice, that you have a set of unquestioned beliefs. . . . You say, but of course, these things are observably true. This is the world we live in, this is life. But if you investigate yourself, observe what lies beneath the lip-service you pay to these notions – for notions they are – you may well discover a layer of yourself that believes quite the opposite. Then what will you do? Stay quiet, I imagine. It takes great courage and persistence to swim against the stream of communal ideas. The stream itself is so much part of daily existence, it is hard to see it for what it is, or understand that it flowed in quite a different direction in other decades.
>
> (Weldon, 1984, p. 32)

The message here is that the fashions and assumptions of every era are to be challenged and held up to continuous examination, whether that examination leads us to believe 'quite the opposite' or not.

We noted in Chapter 2 that intellectual ideas do not come with a sell-by date, and that the value of an idea should be judged by its contribution to our understanding of human affairs. It is not, we think, an unfair analogy to point out that we do not cease to listen to the music of Beethoven once we have heard that of Shostakovitch (perhaps quite the contrary, in fact), or to appreciate traditional jazz once we have heard the playing of Charlie Parker, or to enjoy the paintings of Titian when we have seen those of Picasso. Fashions and styles change, but only in very trivial areas of human experience do they replace what has gone before. Attempts to ensure that new policies totally oust those that they are seeking to replace, therefore, must be recognized as highly suspect and as a form of social manipulation. Such attempts are manifestly concerned to discourage debate and discussion rather than to open them up.

In every age, however, there will be a tendency to discourage debate which ranges far enough to challenge the accepted fashions and assumptions. This of course will be particularly so when there are political reasons for discouraging such questioning. Thus, in the present educational climate in the United Kingdom, attempts are being made by politicians and those employed to carry out their instructions to set parameters for any debate in which teachers and other educationists might wish to engage, and to set those parameters at a point where the discussion of the ideological assumptions which underpin their policies are, or become, 'off-limits'. One of the most effective ways of doing this, and one which is clearly apparent in current practices, is to 'rubbish' those theories which one is seeing as a threat to what one is endeavouring to impose, to 'shout them down' rather than to allow them to be discussed rationally, to be dismissive of them as 'outmoded' or as 'old hat' rather than to debate them seriously, and, in general, to seek to obliterate all forms of discourse in which conflicting ideas are encapsulated. In other words, the concern is to establish a new dominant discourse which will 'determine what counts as true, important, relevant, and what gets spoken' (Cherryholmes, 1987, p. 301), and to clear away all alternative forms of discourse which might get in the way of its establishment by employing what, as we saw in Chapter 4, Stephen Ball has called 'discourses of derision'.

Cherryholmes (op.cit., p. 300) quotes Foucault (1980, p. 200) and his view of the development of 'discursive practices': 'Discursive practices are not purely and simply ways of producing discourse. They are embodied in technical processes, in institutions, in patterns for general behaviour, in forms of transmission and diffusion, and in pedagogical forms which, at once, impose and maintain them'. He goes on (ibid.) to draw our attention to the fact that Foucault argued that it is an inescapable feature of social living that 'discourses are materially produced by specific social, political and economic arrangements. They are not simply idealist constructions'. The rules of a discourse, as he puts it, determine not only 'what can be said' but also 'what must remain unsaid' (op.cit., p. 301). They control 'who can speak with authority and who must listen' (ibid.). And it is thus the dominant discourse which, as we saw above, will 'determine what counts as true, important, relevant, and what gets spoken' (ibid.).

If we apply this kind of analysis – perhaps somewhat simplistically – to the present educational scene in the United Kingdom, we can interpret this as a scenario in which, by the use of those rhetorical devices we considered earlier, a new dominant form of discourse has been politically established and imposed; changes have been brought about in what is seen as 'true, important, relevant' and in 'what gets spoken'; new parameters have been set for educational discourse, parameters which exclude the insights acquired from earlier debates; and the authority to speak with authority on educational matters has been invested in different groups of people – no longer the teachers or even those who have been dubbed 'whingeing academics' but the politicians and the 'educrats'. If one wants concrete evidence of this, one need look no further than the efforts that have been, and are being, made to discourage, even to prevent, teachers, headteachers and local authority advisers from expressing their natural doubts and concerns about current policies, and especially from sharing them with parents.

This kind of analysis and interpretation represents of course a socio- logical account. It has clear links with those many perspectives on society which have emerged under the general heading of 'the politics of knowledge'. And it seems to offer a largely deterministic account of how things inevitably are. Indeed, Cherryholmes (ibid.) also quotes Shapiro (1981, p. 141) as saying, 'It would be appropriate, within his (Foucault's) view of the subject, to reverse the familiar notion that persons make statements, and say that statements make persons'. In other words, it is those forms of discourse which are legitimated which make us what we are and determine what we think rather than vice versa.

Others, however, have suggested that, while this represents a per- fectly reasonable characterization of events such as those currently to be observed in the education system in the United Kingdom, it is not necessary to assume, or accept, its inevitability. For to understand the process is to gain the power and the capability to see beyond it, to recognize it for what it is and thus to step back from it. We saw above, in our discussion of metaphor, that to take a 'constructionist' view is to recognize the subjectivity of metaphor and thus to be forewarned against attempts to use it to manipulate our thinking. Similarly, to recognize the features of discourse we are identifying here is to be able to acknowledge the ideological use of language, and thus to be able to view the world 'reflexively', 'as constructed through experience, linguistic codes, cultural signs, etc.' rather than 'naturalistically', 'as it is' (Slaughter, 1989, p. 264). And to do this, as we also saw above, is to gain 'greater freedom from ideological and linguistic traps, breadth of vision, the ability to "speak one's own words", direct access to fundamental negotiations of meaning' (op.cit., p. 264–5). It enables us to interpret actively and to negotiate meaning instead of 'passively decoding finished structures of meaning' (op.cit., p. 265); and it also enables us to 'feel deeply involved in the process of cultural reconstruction and renewal' (ibid.). In short, it enables people to make statements rather than vice versa.

Another way of putting this is to say that all discourse has its rhetoric and its metaphors, but that we must recognize this if we are to free ourselves from its intellectual limitations. We must adopt an active role in relation to it or else be manipulated by it and by others through it. We must go beyond the notion that the world is 'as it is', that 'this is the world we live in', that 'this is life', and view it 'reflexively', as *constructed* and thus as open to *deconstruction* and *reconstruction*. This is well summed up by Shapiro (1985, p. 19), whom Cherryholmes (1987, p. 310) quotes as saying 'Rather than extending the prevailing control imminent [*sic*] in the language practices of various social agencies, we need to create alternative discursive practices, rhetorical structures that constitute a challenge to existing thought patterns. We need a way of thinking/speaking that gives power no place to hide'.

Finally, it is worth adding that it is for this reason that we have throughout this chapter stressed the importance of a democratic social context for continued, and continuous, change and development. Any concept of democracy will require that, even if social policies cannot be made and implemented by all who are affected by them, they should at least be open to challenge and debate by all so concerned. To both make policy and attempt to implement it by rhetoric, by stealth and manipulation can never be acceptable procedure in a democratic context; it is a procedure which, by definition, belongs in contexts where free and open debate is not tolerated. If we are right, therefore, to claim that current educational policies in the United Kingdom have been made and are being implemented in this kind of way and by these methods, then there are implications here for the very nature and fabric of our society which go well beyond the planning of its education system.

## SUMMARY AND CONCLUSIONS

This chapter has attempted to explore the implications for social change, and especially for change in education policies and practices, of the ideological use of language and of attempts to control and to legitimate forms of discourse. It has addressed these issues both because changes in linguistic and discursive practices have a direct relevance to changes in policy and educational practice and because such changes are important and significant in their own right.

It thus considered at some length the devices most commonly used in rhetoric, the use of metaphor and especially the dangers of 'macroscopic' metaphorical systems and arguments from analogy; and it concluded that, while the subjectivity of language and a 'constructionist' view of metaphor must be accepted, the misuse of these features of language to manipulate and to delimit the thinking of others can never be justified in intellectual or professional discourse and certainly has no place in a democratic social context.

We then examined the main features of the current debate about discourse, and again concluded that, while the ideologies of particular discourses must be recognized, to so recognize them is to be able to free ourselves of their restrictions, and that the attempt to use this feature of discourse to restrict the scope of any debate is again unacceptable in a democratic setting.

Throughout this discussion, although it clearly has relevance for many other aspects of social living, an attempt has been made to point up its significance for current educational policies and practices in the United Kingdom, so that perhaps enough has been said about these, at least for the time being. However, it has emerged very clearly that current policies, and especially the devices which have been employed to implement them, leave a lot to be desired in a society which claims to be democratic, that the non- (even anti-) democratic methods one can detect in current practices have important implications for the development of education and for curriculum change, and, finally, that they also have a crucial significance for continued intellectual advance and for the continued development of democratic forms of living.

# POSTSCRIPT

We set out in this book to offer a comprehensive review of the theory and the practice of curriculum change, to explore some of the different kinds of approach which have been adopted in attempts to bring about such change and to examine some of the theoretical insights which have arisen from reflection on these.

Several issues of general significance have emerged from this review and need to be clearly identified here as we conclude it.

First, it has become very clear that changing the curriculum is a complex undertaking and must be approached with subtlety and sophistication. This is hardly an earth-shattering discovery. For it ought to be readily apparent that all human activities are complex and that all situations of human interaction are rich in nuance, so that any planned intervention in them must be recognized as requiring high levels of sensitivity and skill. It is apparent, however, as we have seen in earlier chapters, that these levels of sensitivity and skill have not always been in evidence when attempts have been made to change the curriculum, and, perhaps more seriously, are far from evident in the sweeping changes currently being attempted by the imposition of the National Curriculum.

Second, these levels of sensitivity and skill can only be attained if we acknowledge the need for a body of appropriate theoretical understandings to underpin our practice of curriculum change, and, further, the need for a continuously interactive, dialectical relationship between theory and practice. It will have become plain from our earlier chapters that the important theoretical perspectives which we elucidated, especially in Chapter 2, have emerged from the practical experiences we outlined in Chapters 3 and 4, and, conversely, that the developments and improvements in practice which we noted were themselves the products of those enhanced theoretical understandings.

Again, in stressing this, we may appear to be stating the obvious, since a dialectical relationship between theory and practice would seem to be an essential prerequisite of any human activity, certainly of any of an intellectual kind, and we have for many years been advocating this as crucial for educational practice in any context. Again, however, self-evident as it may be at the level of reflection, it is too often far from apparent in practice.

Third, a major reason why such a dialectical interaction between theory and practice is necessary is that it is the only route towards narrowing that gap which earlier chapters have also identified between effective change and superficial change, between real or genuine change and change which is either merely cosmetic – a kind of front or window-dressing – or is taken on because it is required or demanded of us rather than because we have recognized it as worthwhile and fully understood its significance. For the latter kinds of change have little or no impact on the substance of education, and, indeed, are more often associated with a reduction in the quality of what is offered to pupils, as evidence from studies in the USA to which we referred in Chapter 3 indicates. The history of education is littered with examples of innovations which, however potentially valuable, were taken on by teachers and others as mere fashions or in response to the demands of others – headteachers, advisers, college tutors – mixed ability teaching, for example, discovery or enquiry learning, learning through play, 'real book' approaches to the teaching of reading, 'new mathematics' and so on. All of these innovations have been highly effective when implemented by teachers who have both understood the theory behind them and have been committed to their educational importance and significance. All of them have equally been disastrous when practised by teachers who lacked both this understanding and this commitment, and who adopted these ideas because in some sense it was, or was felt to be, required of them.

We have long been aware of the importance of the distinction between the 'official' or the 'planned' curriculum and the 'actual' or the 'received', and of the need to seek to close the gap between the two. The quality of education depends entirely on what pupils actually receive in schools and not on the quality of what is offered. And the teacher's professional skill lies in being able to bring the two as closely together as possible. The necessity to continue to work at this task is intensified and heightened by attempts to introduce curriculum change. For such change, if it is to be a proper form of development, should be predicated on the desire to facilitate this *rapprochement*.

If change is to be fully effective, therefore, it will be necessary for teachers to recognize its value, accept the need for it and, perhaps above all, understand the thinking that has prompted it and lies behind it.

It is for this reason that it has also become clear from our review of curriculum change that effective change cannot be brought about by devices which do not seek to involve teachers in a significant way or, worse, by devices which operate on the assumption that they are easy to manipulate or even to fool. We noted in Chapter 5 that, where a proposed innovation is not planned on grounds which lend themselves to clear rational explanation, or where the reasons for it are such that its designers do not wish to state them too clearly, such an innovation cannot be 'sold' in terms of its rationale or value, it can only be imposed by less overt and more subtle forms of manipulation, particularly by the use of the obfuscating devices of rhetoric. In the terminology of one of the theoretical perspectives we considered in Chapter 2, where empirical–rational or normative–re-educative approaches are not available, precisely because there is no empirical or rational case which can be made as part of a normative or re-educative exercise, then recourse must be had to power-coercive strategies, which by definition imply imposition of a suspect innovation on a reluctant and potentially resistant user. It will be plain, however, from all that has been offered in earlier chapters, that such strategies can have only a limited effect, they cannot touch the deep structures of educational provision, except perhaps, as we have also seen, to do harm and damage to them by deflecting teachers from that to which they are professionally committed into that for which they are legally accountable.

If the curriculum is to be planned in such a way as to support the educational advance of all pupils, if it is to be genuinely (and not merely rhetorically) an 'entitlement' curriculum, then it must be planned in such a way as to ensure its continuous development. And changes made to it or innovations introduced into it must contribute to that process of development. They must be evolutionary rather than revolutionary, and they must satisfy the criteria of development we referred to in Chapter 1: they need not necessarily be seen as leading to some nirvana, but they must represent a form of organic growth towards something seen to be, or even merely hoped to be, an improvement on what is already present.

Such development, if it is to be effective and of value, must go hand-in-hand with the professional development of teachers. Without that, curriculum change will be of little lasting value or effect and there can be little expectation of raising the quality of the teaching profession. For the two are inextricably interlinked. It has become a truism to assert that all curriculum development is teacher development. As we suggested earlier, however, the converse is equally true and important. Educational standards can not be raised in any significant or permanent sense by legislation, by schemes of political accountability and appraisal or even by the most skilful use of rhetoric. The only route to continuous and lasting improvement in educational quality is via the professional development of teachers; and that, in turn, entails a proper level of professional responsibility and control.

At root, it has been the aim of this book both to proclaim this view and to contribute to and support the process of its development. It has done both, however, in full recognition that the current climate of education in the United Kingdom and the current approaches both to the school curriculum and to curriculum change fall far short of the model it has sought to offer and elucidate.

# BIBLIOGRAPHY

Acker, S. (1990) Teachers' Culture in an English Primary School: continuity and change. *British Journal of Sociology of Education*, Vol. 11, no. 3, pp. 257–73.

Adams, D., Cornbleth, C. and Plank, D. (1988) Between exhortation and reform – recent US experience with educational change. *Interchange*, Vol. 19, nos. 3/4, pp. 121–34.

Aronowitz, S. and Giroux, H. A. (1986) *Education Under Seige: The Conservative. Liberal and Radical Debate Over Schooling*, Routledge & Kegan Paul, London.

Ball, S. J. (1981) *Beachside Comprehensive: A Case-Study of Secondary Schooling*, Cambridge University Press.

Ball, S. J. (1987) *The Micro-Politics of the School*, Routledge, London.

Ball, S. J. (1989) The micro-politics of the school: baronial politics, in M. Preedy (ed.) op.cit.

Ball, S. J. (1990) *Politics and Policy Making in Education: Exploration in Policy Sociology*, Routledge, London.

Ball, S. J. and Goodson, I. F. (eds.) (1985) *Teachers' Lives and Careers*, The Falmer Press, London.

Banks, L. J. (1969) Curriculum development in Britain, 1963–8, *Journal of Curriculum Studies*, Vol. 1, no. 3, pp. 247–59.

Barker-Lunn, J. C. (1970) *Streaming in the Primary School*, NFER, Slough.

Barton, L. and Walker, S. (eds.) (1981) *Schools, Teachers and Teaching*, The Falmer Press, London.

Becher, A. and Maclure, S. (1978) *The Politics of Curriculum Change*, Hutchinson, London.

Becker, C. L. (1955) What are historical facts?, in R. H. Nash (ed.) (1979) op.cit.

Bennis, W. G., Benne, K. D. and Chin, R. (eds.) (1969) *The Planning of Change*, Holt, Rinehart, & Winston, New York.

Bernstein, B. (1971) On the classification and framing of educational knowledge, in M. F. D. Young (ed.) op.cit.

Blenkin, G. M. and Kelly, A. V. (1981) *The Primary Curriculum*, Harper & Row, London.

Blenkin, G. M. and Kelly, A. V. (eds.) (1983) *The Primary Curriculum in Action*, Harper & Row, London.

Blenkin, G. M. and Kelly, A. V. (1987a) *The Primary Curriculum* (2nd edn), Paul Chapman, London.

Blenkin, G. M. and Kelly, A. V. (eds.) (1987b) *Early Childhood Education: A Developmental Curriculum*, Paul Chapman, London.

Bliss, I. (1990) Intercultural education and the professional knowledge of teachers, *European Journal of Teacher Education*, Vol. 13, no. 3, pp. 141–51.

Bloom, B. S. (ed.) (1956) *Taxonomy for Educational Objectives. 1. Cognitive Domain*, Longman, London.

Blyth, W. A. A. (1974) One development project's awkward thinking about objectives, *Journal of Curriculum Studies*, Vol. 6, no. 2, pp. 99–111.

Bolam, R. (ed.) (1982) *School-Focussed In-Service Training*, Heinemann, London.

Boud, D., Keogh. R. and Walker, D. (1988) *Reflection: Turning Experience Into Learning*, Kogan Page/Nichols Publishing, London.

Broadfoot, P., Osborn, M. with Gilly, M. and Paillet, A. (1988) What professional responsibility means to teachers: national contexts and classroom constants, *British Journal of Sociology of Education*, Vol. 9, no. 3, pp. 265–87.

Bullough Jr., R. V. (1987) Accommodation and tension: teachers, teacher role, and the culture of teaching, in J. Smyth (ed.) op.cit.

Calderhead, J. (ed.) (1987) *Exploring Teachers' Thinking*, Cassell, London.

Calderhead, J. (ed.) (1988) *Teachers' Professional Learning*, The Falmer Press, London.

Carlson, R. (ed.) (1965) *Change Processes in the Public School*, Centre for the Advanced Study of Educational Administration, University of Oregon Press, Eugene, Oregon.

Carr, W. and Kemmis, S. (1986) *Becoming Critical: Education, Knowledge and Action Research*, The Falmer Press, London.

Central Advisory Council for Education (1959) *15–18* (the Crowther Report), HMSO, London.

Central Advisory Council for Education (1967) *Children and Their Primary Schools* (the Plowden Report), HMSO, London.

Cherryholmes, C. H. (1987) A social project for curriculum: post-structural perspectives, *Journal of Curriculum Studies*, Vol. 19, no. 4, pp. 295–316.

Copleston, F. (1966) *A History of Philosophy, Vol. 1, Greece and Rome*, Burn & Oak, London.

Corbett, H. D., Firestone, W. A. and Rossman, G. B. (1987) Resistance to planned change and the sacred in school cultures, *Educational Administration Quarterly*, Vol. 23, no. 4, pp. 36–59.

Corey, S. (1953) *Action Research to Improve School Practice*, Columbia University, New York.

Cox, C. B. and Boyson, R. (eds.) (1977) *Black Papers 1977*, Temple-Smith, London.

Cox, C. B. and Dyson, A. K. (eds.) (1969a) *Fight for Education: A Black Paper*, Critical Quarterly Association, Manchester.

Cox, C. B. and Dyson, A. K. (eds.) (1969b) *Black Paper Two: The Crisis in Education*, Critical Quarterly Association, Manchester.

Cuban, L. (1990) A fundamental puzzle of school reform, in A. Lieberman (ed.) op.cit.

Dalton, T. H. (1988) *The Challenge of Curriculum Innovation: A Study of Ideology and Practice*, The Falmer Press, London.

Dawson, J. (1984) The work of the Assessment of Performance Unit, in M. Skilbeck (ed.) (1984a) op.cit.

Deal, T. E. (1987) The culture of schools, in L. T. Sheive and M. B. Schoenheit (eds.) op.cit.

Deal, T. E. (1990) Reframing reform, *Educational Leadership*, Vol. 47, no. 8, pp. 6–12.

Deal, T. E. and Kennedy, A. A. (1983) Culture and school performance, *Educational Leadership*, Vol. 40, no. 5, pp. 14–15.

Department of Education and Science (1975) *A Language for Life* (the Bullock Report), HMSO, London.

Department of Education and Science (1981) *Review of the Schools Council* (the Trenaman Report), HMSO, London.

Department of Education and Science (1987) *The National Curriculum: A Consultative Document*, HMSO, London.

Department of Education and Science (1988a) *History from 5–16*, Curriculum Matters No. 11, HMSO, London.

Department of Education and Science (1988b) *The Education Reform Act 1988*, HMSO, London.

Department of Education and Science (1989a) *National Curriculum: From Policy to Practice*, HMSO, London.

Department of Education and Science (1989b) *Personal and Social Education from 5–16*, Curriculum Matters no. 11, HMSO, London.

Department of Education and Science/Assessment of Performance Unit (1987) *Design and Technological Activity: A Framework for Assessment*, HMSO, London.

Dewey, J. (1916) *Democracy and Education* (1966 edn), The Free Press, New York.

Doll, W. E. (1989) Foundations for a post-modern curriculum, *Journal of Curriculum Studies*, Vol. 21, no. 3, pp. 243–53.

Doyle, W. and Ponder, G. A. (1977) The practicality ethic in teacher decision-making, *Interchange*, Vol. 8, no. 3, pp. 1–12.

Edwards, G. (1982) Evaluation and accountability in education. Unpublished MA dissertation, University of London.

Edwards, G. (1983) Processes in the secondary school: MACOS and beyond, in G. M. Blenkin and A. V. Kelly (eds.) op.cit.

Edwards, G. (1991) Science and the humanities in M. Watts (ed.) op.cit.

Edwards, G. (1992) A strategy for the curriculum: a response, *Journal of Curriculum Studies*, Vol. 24 (forthcoming).

Edwards, G. and Rideout, P. (1991) *Extending the Horizons of Action Research*, CARN Publication 10C, CARN Publications, Norwich.

Eggleston, J. (1980) *School-Based Curriculum Development in Britain*, Routledge & Kegan Paul, London.

Eisner, E. (1985) *The Art of Educational Evaluation: A Personal View*, The Falmer Press, London.

Elliott, J. (1981) *Action Research: A Framework for Self-Evaluation in Schools*, Schools Council Programme 2 'Teacher–Pupil Interaction and the Quality of Learning' Project, Working paper no. 1.

Elliott, J. (1983) Self-evaluation, professional development and accountability, in M. Galton and B. Moon (eds.) op.cit.

Elliott, J. (1988) *Education in the Shadow of G.E.R.B.I.L.* The Lawrence Stenhouse Memorial Lecture delivered at the British Educational Research Association at the University of East Anglia, September 1988.

Elliott, J. (1991) *Action Research for Educational Change*, Open University Press, Milton Keynes.

Erickson, F. (1987) Conceptions of school culture: an overview, *Educational Administration Quarterly*, Vol. 23, no. 4, pp. 11–24.

Feiman-Nemser, S. and Floden, R. (1986) The culture of teaching, in M. Wittrock (ed.) op.cit.

Flinders, D. J. (1988) Teacher isolation and the new reform, *Journal of Curriculum and Supervision*, Vol. 4, no. 1, pp. 17–29.

Foucault, M. (1980) *Language, Counter-Meaning, Practice*, Cornell University Press, New York.

Fullan, M. (1982) *The Meaning of Educational Change*, OISE Press, Toronto.

Galton, M. and Moon, B. (eds.) (1983) *Changing Schools . . . Changing Curriculum*, Harper & Row, London.

Gibson, R. (1986) *Critical Theory and Education*, Hodder & Stoughton, London.

Giddens, A. (1985) Jurgen Habermas, in Q. Skinner (ed.) op.cit.

Giltin, A. D. (1987) Common school structures and teacher behaviour, in J. Smyth (ed.) op.cit.

Gipps, C. (1984) An evaluation of the Assessment of Performance Unit, in M. Skilbeck (ed.) (1984a) op.cit.

Giroux, H. A. (1989) *Schooling for Democracy: Critical Pedagogy in the Modern Age*, Routledge, London.

Goodlad, J. I. (1987a) Towards a healthy ecosystem, in J. I. Goodlad (ed.) (1987b) op.cit.

Goodlad, J. I. (ed.) (1987b) *The Ecology of School Renewal*, University of Chicago Press.

Goodson, I. F. (1981) Becoming an academic subject: patterns of explanation and evolution, *British Journal of Sociology of Education*, Vol. 2, no. 2, pp. 163–80.

Goodson, I. F. (1983) Subjects for study: aspects of a social history of curriculum, *Journal of Curriculum Studies*, Vol. 15, no. 4, pp. 391–408.

Goodson, I. F. (ed.) (1985) *Social Histories of the Secondary Curriculum: Subjects for Study*, The Falmer Press, London.

Goodson, I. F. (1987) *School Subjects and Curriculum Change*, The Falmer Press, London.

Goodson, I. F. (1991) Sponsoring the teacher's voice: teachers' lives and teacher development, *Cambridge Journal of Education*, Vol. 21, no. 1, pp. 35–45.

Goodson, I. F. and Ball, S. J. (eds.) (1984) *Defining the Curriculum: Histories and Ethnographies*, The Falmer Press, London.

Goodson, I. F. and Walker, R. (1991) *Biography, Identity and Schooling: Episodes in Educational Research*, The Falmer Press, London.

Gross, N., Giacquinta, J. B. and Bernstein, M. (1971) *Implementing Organizational Innovations*, Harper & Row, New York.

Grundy, S. (1987) *Curriculum: Product or Praxis?*, The Falmer Press, London.

Habermas, J. (1976) *Legitimation Crisis*, Heinemann, London.

Hargreaves, A. (1981) Contrastive rhetoric and extremist talk, in L. Barton and S. Walker (eds.) op.cit.

Hargreaves, A. (1982) The rhetoric of school-centred innovation, *Journal of Curriculum Studies*, Vol. 14, no. 3, pp. 251–66.

Hargreaves, A. (1984) Experience counts, theory doesn't: how teachers talk about their work, *Sociology of Education*, Vol. 57, pp. 244–54.

Hargreaves, A. (1989) *Curriculum and Assessment Reform*, Open University Press, Milton Keynes.

Hargreaves, A. (1990a) Individualism and individuality: reinterpreting the teacher culture. Paper presented at AERA, Boston, April 1990.

Hargreaves, A. (1990b) Contrived Collegiality. Paper presented at the XIIth meeting of the International Sociological Association, Madrid, 9–13 July 1990.

Hargreaves, D. H. (1982) The occupational culture of teachers, in P. Woods (ed.) op.cit.

Harris, A., Lawn, M. and Prescott, W. (eds.) (1975) *Curriculum Innovation*, Croom Helm with Open University Press, London.

Harvey, D. (1989) *The Condition of Postmodernity. An Enquiry Into the Origins of Cultural Change*, Basil Blackwell, Oxford.

Havelock, R. G. (1971) The utilization of educational research and development, *British Journal of Educational Technology*, Vol. 2, no. 2, pp. 84–97. Reprinted in T. Horton and P. Raggatt (eds.) (1982) op.cit.

Havelock, R. G. (1973) *The Change Agent's Guide to Innovation in Education*, Educational Technology Publications, New Jersey.

Heckman, P. (1987) Understanding school culture, in J. I. Goodlad (ed.) (1987b) op.cit.

Henderson, E. and Perry, W. (1981) *Change and Developments in Schools: Case Studies in the Management of School-Focused Inservice Education*, McGraw-Hill, London.

Hicks, G. (1976) Design studies in education. Unpublished M. Phil. thesis, University of London.

Holly, M. L. (1991) Personal and professional learning: on teaching and self-knowledge. Paper presented at the Classroom Action Research Network International Conference at Nottingham University, 21 April 1991.

Holly, P. (1984) The institutionalization of action research in schools, *Cambridge Journal of Education*, Vol. 14, no. 2, pp. 5–18.

Holt, M. (1981) *Evaluating the Evaluators*, Hodder & Stoughton, London.

Holt, M. (1987) *Judgement, Planning and Educational Change*, Harper & Row, London.

Holt, M. (1990) Managing curriculum change in a comprehensive school: conflict, compromise and deliberation, *Journal of Curriculum Studies*, Vol. 22, no. 2, pp. 137–48.

Hopkins, D. (1990) *Evaluation for School Development*, Open University Press, Milton Keynes.

Hopkins, D. and Wideen, M. (eds.) (1984) *Alternative Perspectives on School Improvement*, The Falmer Press, London.

Hord, S. (1987) *Evaluating Educational Innovation*, Croom Helm, London.

Horkheimer, M. (1947) *The Eclipse of Reason.*

Horton, T. and Raggatt, P. (eds.) (1982) *Challenge and Change in the Curriculum*, Hodder & Stoughton, London.

House, E. R. (1974) *The Politics of Educational Innovation*, McCutchan Publishing Corporation, Berkeley, California.

House, E. R. (1979) Technology versus craft: a ten year perspective on innovation, *Journal of Curriculum Studies*, Vol. 11, no. 1, pp. 1–15.

House, E. R. (1981) Three perspectives on innovation, in R. Lehming and M. Kane (eds.) op.cit.

Hoyle, E. (1969) How does the curriculum change? 2. Systems and strategies, *Journal of Curriculum Studies*, Vol. 1, no. 3, pp. 230–9.

Hoyle, E. (1975) The creativity of the school in Britain, in A. Harris *et al.* (eds.) op.cit.

Hoyle, E. (1982) Micropolitics of educational organizations, *Educational Management and Administration*, Vol. 10, pp. 87–98.

Huberman, M. (1978) Microanalysis of innovation implementation at the school level. Unpublished paper, University of Geneva.

Huberman, M. (1988) Teacher careers and school improvement, *Journal of Curriculum Studies*, Vol. 20, no. 2, pp. 119–32.

Humble, S. and Simons, H. (1978) *From Council to Classroom: An Evaluation of the Diffusion of the Humanities Curriculum Project*, Macmillan Education, London.

Kelly, A. V. (1977) *The Curriculum: Theory and Practice*, Harper and Row, London.

Kelly, A. V. (1986) *Knowledge and Curriculum Planning*, Harper & Row, London.

Kelly, A. V. (1989) *The Curriculum: Theory and Practice* (3rd edn), Paul Chapman, London.

Kelly, A. V. (1990) *The National Curriculum: A Critical Review*, Paul Chapman, London.

Kemmis, S. (1988) Action research and the politics of reflection, in D. Boud *et al.* (ed.) op.cit.

Kirk, D. (1988) Ideology and school-centred innovation: a case study and critique, *Journal of Curriculum Studies*, Vol. 20, no. 5, pp. 449–64.

Knight, P. (1985) The practice of school-based curriculum development, *Journal of Curriculum Studies*, Vol. 17, no. 1, pp. 37–48.

Kyriacou, C. (1987) Teacher stress and burnout: an international review, *Educational Research*, Vol. 29, no. 2, pp. 145–52.

Lawton, D. (1980) *The Politics of the School Curriculum*, Routledge & Kegan Paul, London.

Lawton, D. (1987) Fundamentally flawed, *Times Educational Supplement*, 18 September.

Lawton, D. and Chitty, C. (eds.) (1988) *The National Curriculum*, Bedford Way Paper 33, Institute of Education, London.

Lauer, R. H. and Lauer, J. C. (1976) The experience of change: tempo and stress, in G. K. Zollschan and W. Hirsch (eds.) op.cit.

Lee, V. and Zeldin, D. (eds.) (1982) *Planning the Curriculum*, Hodder & Stoughton, Sevenoaks.

Lehming, R. and Kane, M. (eds.) (1981) *Improving Schools: Using What We Know*, Sage, Beverly Hills, CA.

Lieberman, A. (1986) Collaborative work, *Educational Leadership*, Vol. 43, no. 5, pp. 4–8.

Lieberman, A. (ed.) (1990) *Schools as Collaborate Cultures: Creating the Future Now*, The Falmer Press, London.

Lieberman, A. and Miller, L. (1990) Teacher development in professional practice schools, *Teachers College Record*, Vol. 92, no. 1, pp. 105–22.

Lieberman, A. and Rozenholtz, S. (1987) The road to school improvement: barriers and bridges, in J. I. Goodlad (ed.) (1987b) op.cit.

Little, W. A. (1990) The persistence of privacy: autonomy and initiative in teachers' professional relationships, *Teachers College Record*, Vol. 94, no. 1, pp. 509–36.

Lortie, D. C. (1975) *Schoolteacher: A Sociological Study*, University of Chicago Press.

McCutcheon, G. and Jung, B. (1990) Alternative perspectives on action research, *Theory Into Practice*, Vol. XXIX, no. 3, pp. 144–51.

McMahon, A., Bolam, R., Abbott, R. and Holly, P. (1984) *Guidelines for Review and Internal Development in Schools: Secondary School Handbook*, Longman, York.

McNiff, J. (1988) *Action Research: Principles and Practice*, Macmillan Education, London.

MacDonald, B. and Rudduck, J. (1971) Curriculum research and development projects: barriers to success, *British Journal of Educational Psychology*, Vol. 41, part 2, pp. 148–54.

MacDonald, B. and Walker, R. (1976) *Changing the Curriculum*, Open Books, London.

MacIntyre, A. (1985) *After Virtue: A Study in Moral Theory*, Duckworth, London.

Mack, J. (1976) Assessing schools, *New Society*, 25 November.

Malkus, U. C., Feldman, D. H. and Gardner, H. (1988) Dimensions of the mind in early childhood, in A. D. Pellegrini (ed.) op.cit.

Marris, P. (1974) *Loss and Change*, Routledge & Kegan Paul, London.

Matthews, J. C. and Leece, J. R. (1976) *Schools Council Examinations Bulletin 33: Examinations: Their Use in Curriculum Evaluation and Development*, Evans/Methuen, London.

Measor, L. (1985) Critical incidents in the classroom: identities, choices and careers, in S. J. Ball and I. F. Goodson (eds.) op.cit.

162 *Bibliography*

Miles, M. B. (ed.) (1964) *Innovation in Education*, Teachers College, Columbia University, New York.

Miles, M. B. (1965) Planned change and organizational health; figure and ground, in R. Carlson (ed.) op.cit. Reprinted in A. Harris *et al.* (eds.) (1975) op.cit.

Nash, R. H. (ed.) (1979) *Ideas of History*, E. P. Dutton, New York.

National Curriculum Council (1990) *Curriculum Guidance 3 – The Whole Curriculum*, NCC, London.

Nias, J. (1989) Refining the 'cultural perspective', *Cambridge Journal of Education*, Vol. 19, no. 2, pp. 143–6.

Nisbet, J. (1974) *Creativity of the School*, CERI/OECD, Paris.

Nowell-Smith, P. H. (1954) *Ethics*, Penguin, Harmondsworth.

Oliver, D. W. with Gershman, K. W. (1989) *Education, Modernity and Fractured Meaning: Towards a Process Theory of Teaching and Learning*, State University of New York Press, Albany.

Olson, J. K. (1980) Teachers' constructs and curriculum change, *Journal of Curriculum Studies*, Vol. 12, no. 1, pp. 1–11.

Olson, J. K. and Eaton, S. (1987) Curriculum change and the classroom order, in J. Calderhead (ed.) op.cit.

Ortony, A. (ed.) (1979a) *Metaphor and Thought*, Cambridge University Press.

Ortony, A. (1979b) Metaphor: a multidimensional problem, in A. Ortony (ed.) op.cit.

Patriarca, L. A. and Buchmann, M. (1983) Conceptual development and curriculum change: or is it rhetoric and fantasy, *Journal of Curriculum Studies*, Vol. 15, no. 4, pp. 409–23.

Pellegrini, A. D. (1988) *Psychological Bases for Early Education*, John Wiley, Chichester and New York.

Peters, R. S. (1966) *Authority, Responsibility and Education*, George Allen & Unwin, London.

Plaskow, M. (ed.) (1985) *The Life and Death of the Schools Council*, The Falmer Press, London.

Ponder, G. A. and Doyle, W. (1977) The practicality ethic in teacher decision-making, *Interchange*, Vol. 8, no. 3, pp. 1–12.

Popper, K. (1945) *The Open Society and its Enemies, Vols. 1 and 2*, Routledge & Kegan Paul.

Porter, A. C. (1987) Teacher collaboration: new partnerships to attack old problems, *Phi Delta Kappan*, Vol. 69, pp. 147–52.

Preedy, M. (ed.) (1989) *Approaches to Curriculum Management*, Open University Press, Milton Keynes.

Prescott, W. and Hoyle, E. (1976) *Innovation: Problems and Possibilities*, Open University course E203 Units 22 and 23, Open University Press, Milton Keynes.

Pudwell, C. (1983) Public examinations and a process model of curriculum, *Curriculum*, Vol. 4, no. 2.

Reid, K., Hopkins, D. and Holly, P. (1987) *Towards the Effective School*, Basil Blackwell, Oxford.

Richardson, E. (1973) *The Teacher, the School and the Task of Management*, Heinneman, London.

Rogers, C. R. (1983) *Freedom to Learn for the 80's*, Charles E. Merrill, Columbus, Ohio.

Rogers, E. M. (1962) *Diffusion of Innovation*, The Free Press, New York.

Rosario, J. R. (1986) Excellence, school culture, and lessons in utility: another case against simplistic views of educational change, *Journal of Curriculum Studies*, Vol. 18, no. 1, pp. 31–43.

Rosenholtz, S. J. (1987) Political myths about education reform: lessons from research on teaching, *Phi Delta Kappan*, Vol. 166, no. 5, pp. 349–55.

Rosenholtz, S. J. (1990) Education reform strategies: will they increase teacher commitment?, in A. Lieberman (ed.) op.cit.

Ross, D. H. (1958) *Administration for Adaptability: A Source Book for Drawing Together the Results of More than 150 Individual Studies Related to the Question of Why and How Schools Improve*, Metropolitan School Study Council, New York.

Rossman, G. B., Corbett, H. D. and Firestone, W. A. (1988) *Change and Effectiveness in Schools*, State University NY Press, New York.

Rudduck, J. (1984) Introducing innovation to pupils, in D. Hopkins and M. Wideen (ed.) (1984) op.cit.

Rudduck, J. (1986a) Curriculum change: management or meaning? *School Organization*, Vol. 6, no. 1, pp. 107–14.

Rudduck, J. (1986b) *Understanding Curriculum Change*, Division of Education, University of Sheffield.

Rudduck, J. (1988) The ownership of change as a basis for teachers' professional learning, in J. Calderhead (ed.) op.cit.

Rudduck, J. and Kelly, P. (1976) *The Dissemination of Curriculum Development*, NFER, Windsor.

Ryan, A. (1965) Freedom, *Philosophy*, Vol. XL, no. 152.

Sarason, S. B. (1982) *The Culture of the School and the Problem of Change* (2nd edn), Allyn & Bacon, Boston.

Schon, D. A. (1971) *Beyond the Stable State*, Temple Smith, London.

Schon, D. A. (1983) *The Reflective Practitioner: How Professionals Think in Action*, Temple Smith, London.

Schon, D. A. (1987) *Educating the Reflective Practitioner*, Jossey-Bass Publishers, San Francisco.

School Examinations and Assessment Council/Evaluation and Monitoring Unit (1991a) *Learning Through Design and Technology: The APU Model*, Leaflet No. 1, HMSO, London.

School Examinations and Assessment Council/Evaluation and Monitoring Unit (1991b) *The Assessment of Performance in Design and Technology*, HMSO, London.

Schools Council (1975) *The First Ten Years: 1964–1974*, Schools Council, London.

Schools Council (1978) *Impact and Take-Up Project: A First Interim Report*, Schools Council, London.

Schools Council (1980) *The Next Three Years: 1980–1983*, Schools Council, London.

Secondary Schools Examinations Council (1960) *Secondary School Examinations other than the GCE* (the Beloe Report), HMSO, London.

Shapiro, M. (1981) Post-structuralist political pedagogy, *News for Teachers of Political Science*, no. 44.

Sheive, L. T. and Schoenheit, M. B. (eds.) (1987) *Leadership: Examining the Elusive*, ASCD Yearbook 1987, Association for Supervision and Curriculum Development, Alexandria, VA.

Shibutani, T. (1961) *Society and Personality*, Prentice-Hall, Englewood Cliffs.

Shipman, M. (1973) The impact of a curriculum project, *Journal of Curriculum Studies*, Vol. 5, no. 1, pp. 47–54.

Sikes, P. J. (1985) The life cycle of the teacher, in S. J. Ball and I. F. Goodson, (eds.) (1985) op.cit.

Sikes, P. J., Measor, L. and Woods, P. (eds.) (1985) *Teacher Careers: Crises and Continuities*, The Falmer Press, London.

Simons, H. (1987) *Getting to Know Schools in a Democracy: The Politics and Process of Evaluation*, The Falmer Press, London.

Simons, H. (1988) Teacher professionalism and the national curriculum, in D. Lawton and C. Chitty (eds.) op.cit.

Skilbeck, M. (1975) School-based curriculum development and teacher education. Mimeographed paper. Reprinted in V. Lee and D. Zeldin (eds.) (1982) op.cit.

Skilbeck, M. (1984a) *School-Based Curriculum Development*, Harper & Row, London.

Skilbeck, M. (ed.) (1984b) *Evaluating the Curriculum in the Eighties*, Hodder & Stoughton, London.

Skilbeck, M. (1984c) *Readings in School-Based Curriculum Development*, Harper & Row, London.

Skinner, B. F. (1968) *The Technology of Teaching*, Appleton-Century-Croft, New York.

Skinner, Q. (ed.) (1985) *The Return of Grand Theory in Human Sciences*, Cambridge University Press.

Slaughter, R. A. (1989) Cultural reconstruction in the post-modern world, *Journal of Curriculum Studies*, Vol. 21, no. 3, pp. 255–70.

Smyth, J. (ed.) (1987) *Educating Teachers: Changing the Nature of Pedagogical Knowledge*, The Falmer Press, London.

Sparkes, A. C. (1987) Strategic rhetoric: a constraint in changing the practice of teachers, *British Journal of Sociology of Education*, Vol. 8, no. 1, pp. 37–54.

Sparkes, A. C. (1989) Towards an understanding of the personal costs and rewards involved in teacher initiated innovations, *Educational Management and Administration*, Vol. 17, pp. 100–108.

Stein, M. K. and Wang, M. C. (1988) Teacher development and school improvement: the process of teacher change, *Teaching and Teacher Education*, Vol. 4, no. 2, pp. 171–87.

Stenhouse, L. (1975) *An Introduction to Curriculum Research and Development*, Heinemann, London.

Stenhouse, L. (1979) Research as a basis for teaching, in L. Stenhouse, (1983b) op.cit.

Stenhouse, L. (1980a) Curriculum research and the art of the teacher, *Curriculum*, Vol. 1, no. 1, pp. 40–4. Also in L. Stenhouse (1983b) op.cit.

Stenhouse, L. (ed.) (1980b) *Curriculum Research and Development in Action*, Heinemann, London.

Stenhouse, L. (1983a) The legacy of the curriculum movement, in M. Galton and B. Moon (eds) op.cit.

Stenhouse, L. (1983b) *Authority, Education and Emancipation*, Heinemann, London.

Stenhouse, L. (1984) Artistry and teaching: the teacher as focus of research and development, in D. Hopkins and M. Wideen (eds.) (1984) op.cit.

Storm, M. (1989a) World view, *Teacher*, 1 May, pp. 12–14.

Storm, M. (1989b) Geography and the national curriculum, *Teaching Geography*, Vol. 14, no. 3, pp. 103–4.

Taba, H. (1962) *Curriculum Development: Theory and Practice*, Harcourt, Brace & World, New York.

Tom, A. R. (1980) Teaching as a moral craft: a metaphor for teaching and teacher education, *Curriculum Inquiry*, Vol. 10, no. 3, pp. 317–23.

Tripp, D. (1990) Socially critical action research, *Theory Into Practice*, Vol. XXIX, no. 3, pp. 158–66.

Trumbull, D. J. (1989) Computer-generated challenges to school culture: one teacher's story, *Journal of Curriculum Studies*, Vol. 21, no. 5, pp. 457–69.

Tyler R. W. (1949) *Basic Principles of Curriculum and Instruction*, University of Chicago Press, Chicago.

van Manen, M. (1990) Beyond assumptions: shifting the limits of action research, *Theory Into Practice*, Vol. XXIX, no. 3, pp. 152–7.

Walker, S. and Barton, L. (eds.) (1987) *Changing Policies, Changing Teachers: New Directions for Schooling?* Open University Press, Milton Keynes.

Watts, M. (ed.) (1991) *Science in the National Curriculum*, Cassell, London.

Webb, R. B. and Ashton, P. T. (1987) Teacher motivation and the conditions of teaching: a call for ecological reform, in S. Walker and L. Barton (eds.) op.cit.

Weick, K. E. (1976) Educational organizations as loosely coupled systems, *Administrative Science Quarterly*, Vol. 21, pp. 1–19. Reprinted in A. Westoby (ed.) (1988) op.cit.

Weldon, F. (1984) *Letters to Alice*, Coronet Books, Hodder & Stoughton, London.

Westoby, A. (ed.) (1988) *Culture and Power in Educational Organizations*, Open University Press, Milton Keynes.

Wilson, J. (1963) *Thinking with Concepts*, Cambridge University Press.

Wittrock, M. (ed.) (1986) *Handbook of Research on Teaching* (3rd edn), American Educational Research Association, Washington DC.

Woods, P. (ed.) (1982) *Teacher Strategies*, Croom Helm, London.

Young, M. F. D. (1971) An approach to the study of curricula as socially organised knowledge in M. F. D. Young op.cit.

Young, M. F. D. (ed.) (1971) *Knowledge and Control*, Collier Macmillan, London.

Zaltman, G., Floria, D. H. and Sikorski, L. A. (1977) *Dynamic Educational Change: Models Strategies, Tactics and Management*, The Free Press, New York.

Zollschan, G. K. and Hirsch, W. (eds.) (1976) *Social Change: Explorations, Diagnoses, and Conjectures*, John Wiley & Sons, New York.

# AUTHOR INDEX

*Page numbers in italics refer to bibliographical details*

# SUBJECT INDEX